FINDING TRUTH WITH MICHAEL

A Memoir of Friendship, Faith, and First Love

DARLS CENTOLA

© 2026, Darls Centola. All rights reserved.
Published by Awe & Wonder, Los Angeles, California
FindingTruthWithMichael.com

Finding Truth with Michael:
A Memoir of Friendship, Faith, and First Love

ISBN: 979-8-9937264-1-0 (paperback)
ISBN: 979-8-9937264-0-3 (eBook)
ISBN: 979-8-9937264-2-7 (audiobook)
Library of Congress Control Number: 2025927843

This is a true story based on the author's memories and personal experiences. While every effort has been made to portray events and individuals accurately, some names and identifying details have been changed to protect privacy. As with any memoir, recollections may reflect the author's perspective and the passage of time.

Without limiting the rights under copyright reserved above, no part of this publication may be reproduced, stored in or introduced into a retrieval system, or transmitted in any form or by any means (electronic, mechanical, photocopying, recording, or otherwise, whether now or hereafter known), without the prior written permission of both the copyright owner and the above publisher of this book, except by a reviewer who wishes to quote brief passages in connection with a review written for insertion in a magazine, newspaper, broadcast, website, blog, or other outlet in conformity with United States and International Fair Use or comparable guidelines to such copyright exceptions.

For those navigating the complexities of religious trauma, faith deconstruction, and the aftermath of adverse religious experiences.

To the ones who have left high-demand systems, broken free from spiritual abuse, and unlearned what they were told was absolute.

And to those who walk alongside them, offering understanding, support, and the courage to rebuild.

"Darls was my first and only friend outside the family, and I treasured the time we spent together. One of the few girls in our school not in awe of Michael, she treated him as just another kid, which he really appreciated."
— La Toya Jackson
La Toya: Growing Up in the Jackson Family

Michael J. and I have been spending quite a bit of time together... I adore Michael; I think I'm growing to love him. But not boyfriend-type love. Just best-friend type. He feels the same about me, too. I can tell. His personality is one of the best I've ever known.
— Darls Centola
Journal entry, January 25, 1974

CONTENTS

Preface i

PART ONE: THE PROMISE 1
Principal's Office, 1971 3
Forbidden 6
Getaway Van 12
Playing Hooky 21
Cal Prep 26
The Jacksons Arrive 30
Family Dinner 36
La Toya 40
Recruiting for Jehovah 45
First Bible Study 51
The Truth That Leads to Eternal Life 55
Heathen Weed 66
Baptism 69
Soul Train 74
One More for the Flock 84
Armageddon 89
In Service 93
Kingdom Hall 98
At Home with the Jacksons 102
Llama Linda 111
Under Surveillance 121

Going Away Gift 126
First Car Freedom 132
Summer of '75 139

PART TWO: THE VOICE INSIDE **145**
Dinner Party 147
Fornication 154
Change of Course 173
Playboy Mansion 177
Tap Dancing 183
A New Elder in Town 192
Decided 197
Telling Michael 201
The Letter 203
Spiritual Abuse 206
I Was a Watchtower Slave 213

PART THREE — WHAT REMAINS **215**
Disfellowshipped 217
Solo Flight 221
Clandestine Reunions 224
Chains Falling Off 229
Flying the Coop 231
The Wiz 234
Oh, God 237
Children of Many Lands 241
The Farewell 245
Epilogue 250

PART FOUR: PHOTO ALBUM **255**

Acknowledgments 283
Resources for Adverse Religious Experiences 285
About the Author 289

PREFACE

The two Elders sat me in a small, nondescript office, the same one where the baptism questions were posed.

"Sister Darls, can you tell us a little about how you conduct your studies with Michael?" Brother Long asked.

I explained that we used the Bible study aid, *The Truth that Leads to Eternal Life*, just as I did with Tina, and that we took turns reading the paragraphs and then discussed the important points. I didn't volunteer that we did more talking and joking than actual Bible studying.

"We know you're newly baptized and a dedicated servant of Jehovah," Brother Long said. "You have the knowledge required, but it's important to understand certain issues might arise due to the high-profile nature of the Jacksons. We'll occasionally provide you with guidance and oversight."

I felt special that they were acknowledging my qualifications and abilities. At the same time, I was anxious to leave the office. Typically, being called into that office alone with the Elders meant a reprimand, and I didn't want anyone to get the wrong impression—especially after what had happened to Ken Lewis.

After coming out of the Elders' private chambers, I went outside and found Michael under a tree. With one hand gripping the trunk, he swung, circling close to me and then farther away, each time moving in a bit more. He came up to my face and then swung back. He was so close; I could feel his breath on my mouth. My knees weakened. *Is he going to kiss me right here in the parking lot of the Kingdom Hall?*

PART ONE
THE
PROMISE

> Michael is my best friend, as far as I'm concerned. I like him more than any other friend.
>
> — Journal entry, February 20, 1974

> Michael is the one who opened my eyes about nature. He appreciates it so much.
>
> — Journal entry, March 13, 1975

> Today was my last study with Michael for a few weeks. He's going to Vegas. It was a great study. It was so juicy and full of good points. He came with me to the bus stop and we talked for a while. I enjoy his companionship so much. He always makes me feel much better. He told me about this butterfly that lives for only one day, and compared it with one day to Jehovah is a thousand years to us.
>
> — Journal entry, April 4, 1975

PRINCIPAL'S OFFICE, 1971

My stomach was in knots—not because I was in the principal's office, but because my mom was on her way. My crime: refusing to salute the flag. As a recent Jehovah's Witness convert, I followed my convictions with fervor, but I hadn't expected trouble. Being right with God, I was learning, came at a cost.

The secretary mumbled something about suspension. I stared at the second hand on the clock—it moved so slowly; it seemed to tick backward.

The inside of the principal's office door was covered in mesh wire. Was this added metal barrier meant to keep students out or in?

Since moving to L.A., I was stuck at a massive, crumbling public school that looked—and felt—like a prison. Girls in my class threatened to beat me up. That week, they'd laughed as I boarded the bus, yelling, "Don't forget your Bible!"

Getting into this kind of trouble would never have happened before I joined the Jehovah's Witnesses. I always tried to fly under my mother's radar. Now I was willing to face both her and the school authorities because I felt I had something to stand up for.

As a Jehovah's Witness I was the good girl, the rule follower. My two oldest sisters, Angela and Lisa, smoked pot, and cigarettes, and went to parties with no curfew. Their bedroom reeked and sometimes pot smoke filled the hallway. It seemed like our mother had given up on them.

Perhaps hypocrisy was part of the reason—our mother used marijuana herself and thought she had it well hidden, but Angela and Lisa had been stealing it from her closet.

I expected my mother to arrive in a fit of rage—but to my surprise, her anger wasn't aimed at me.

"I'm Darls' mother, June Terry," she barked, storming in like she owned the place. Purple silk bell-bottoms clung to her long legs, and a ruffled white satin blouse flashed beneath a waterfall of colorful earrings. Her pink Chanel lipstick matched her sharp tone. Her hair, shellacked into a perfect upward sweep, didn't move an inch as she loomed over the secretary.

"I need to speak with the principal. Now!"

The secretary stood up and reached to open the office door at the same moment the principal swung it open.

"What's all the shouting about?" She looked directly at my mother.

"My daughter has the right to refuse to salute the flag," my mother said. "She is acting as a conscientious objector and demonstrating her rights as a US citizen."

I was baffled. *Was my mom really defending my right to be a Jehovah's Witness?*

The principal kept her cool. "I understand, Mrs. Centola, but we have certain standards, values, and expectations of conduct in our classrooms."

"The First Amendment gives her the right to freedom of speech and freedom of religion. This kind of political oppression is the very reason students are being beaten with sticks by the cops for protesting this goddamn lie of a war."

The principal tried to interject, but my mother steamrolled ahead with a ten-minute rant, even threatening to go to the press. At last, the principal gave in.

"As long as Darls stands during the pledge," she relented, "we can overlook her resistance."

"But I was standing!" I finally found my voice. Jehovah's Witnesses stood out of respect—we just didn't salute. I couldn't wait to share this story with the others. Being singled out for my beliefs felt like proof of my devotion.

My mother grabbed my hand and led me out. I left with my head held high—at least for the moment.

FORBIDDEN

It was at least 100 degrees in the San Fernando Valley, and the asphalt was practically melting. My mother's grip on me tightened as we crossed the parking lot.

"How dare you screw up my day with your goddamn idiotic religious antics!" she snapped.

I slipped into the Cadillac and the dark leather seat burned the back of my thighs.

My mother reached over, grabbed my cheek, and gave it an angry yank. "How could you be so stupid?"

I said nothing, knowing anything I might say would only aggravate her more. Our address was in Sherman Oaks, south of Ventura Boulevard—the local code for "high class." Ventura Boulevard straddled the San Fernando Valley like a social thermometer. South of the Boulevard signified success; north of the Boulevard, something less.

Our family had moved abruptly from Northern to Southern California after my parents' modeling school burned to the ground in a fire. They refused to answer any of our questions about the fire. My father took us five kids on a road trip to Los Angeles while my mother stayed behind to deal with the fire investigators. Thanks to her negotiation skills and some fire insurance money, my parents were able to purchase an extravagant four-bedroom house in the hills with a view of the city below. They'd since opened a new modeling school—one more in their chain of businesses.

My mother slammed on the brakes at a red light and put her arm out; I winced, expecting to be hit, before realizing she'd done it to protect me.

"If you think you're getting hit, then I may as well." She reached out to slap me; I pulled away, and her nails grazed my cheek. "I'd rather you be a drug addict on the street than in that mind-controlling cult of a religion," she said, "and I forbid you to go to those god-thumping meetings ever again, so don't even ask!"

She screeched to a halt in the driveway.

I jumped out of the car and ran to my room to find my sister Susie. We needed to act fast, because we had plans to go to the Kingdom Hall that evening.

I shared a bedroom with Susie, who was two years older than me. The wallpaper, bedspread, and sheets all had the same matching orange and yellow floral print pattern.

Susie was facing the mirrored closet door, gracefully practicing pliés. She was willowy and tall with long, straight golden-brown hair, while the rest of us kids had dark, curly hair. We always teased her about being the adopted child. Like our mother, she was obsessed with staying thin. She also wanted to follow in her footsteps—Mom was a former dancer.

Adolescence had made me curvier, and that meant I couldn't meet my mother's standards.

With my parents being in the glamor business and living in Los Angeles, I thought that appearance was everything. My mother was a size six with a Barbie doll figure. She was so weight-obsessed, she spent two days a week on a diet of scrambled eggs, steak, and tomatoes. "What are we going to do?" I pleaded. "Mom said no more meetings and no more Jehovah's Witnesses!"

"We can pretend we're going to the library to study," she said. "I told Dad we needed to go this week, so let's make it tonight."

I considered this. "What about Tina and Phil? They're picking us up at six-thirty and they can't come to the house." Tina and Phil were our Bible study mentors. "I'll call and tell them to wait for us at the bottom of our street," Susie replied nonchalantly.

I was a nervous wreck. Lying felt so wrong. I changed into my Kingdom Hall clothes and headed to the kitchen.

Mom was at the counter, slamming cupboards and yelling at Dad about their latest investor. A gallon of Kamchatka vodka stood next to her crystal tumbler, ice clinking with each sip. Her cigarette burned into a perfect log of ashes in the Caesars Palace ashtray. "You're making promises we can't keep, Frank. Look at the numbers. I can't possibly sell that many modeling courses."

My father was reading the *Wall Street Journal* while the TV announced the five o'clock news. "That asshole Nixon is sending more young boys to slaughter," he grumbled. The phone rang and I answered.

Holding my hand over the mouthpiece, I whispered, "It's the Diners Club credit card company asking for Frank Parker."

Bill collection calls were frequent at our house. The caller typically asked for Frank Parker, Beaumont, Wilson, Williams, Terry, or Toma, and included names of companies that didn't exist.

My mother yanked the phone from my hand. "*Meee* the maid, no *speeeek* English," she said, and slammed it down. Without missing a beat, she went back to the kitchen and lit another cigarette, drawing so hard it produced an inch-long ash. She grabbed her drink with the other hand and took a long sip with her eyes closed, smoke meeting the ice in her glass. A box of Uncle Ben's rice fell on the floor, spilling everywhere.

"What moron put the rice away like this?!" she barked. "Darlsy, get the broom."

I grabbed it quickly.

"What are you wearing?" she snapped. "You look like a pilgrim."

"I was just trying on some clothes for school tomorrow, but they don't fit right," I lied. "I'll change."

As I raced down the hall toward my bedroom, I smelled the pot smoke escaping from Angela and Lisa's bedroom across the hall while Neil Young blared from their stereo. *They're committing a felony right in our house*, I thought, *while I'm being punished for wanting to be a CHRISTIAN.*

Susie was lying on the bed in her bra and underwear, studying her face in a hand mirror.

"You could come help with dinner, you know," I mumbled.

She smiled mischievously and gave me her good news: She'd been able to reach Tina and change the plan for tonight. We were to meet them down the hill, where they'd be waiting in their van.

"Well, we'd better dress like we're going to the library, or Mom might figure out where we're really going," I reminded her.

I changed into a pair of jeans and a T-shirt and ran back to the kitchen.

"There will be no more of this Jehovah's Witness nonsense after today," Mom announced at the dinner table.

I was in the seat to her right and my younger brother, Mikey, was to her left. Susie sat closest to my father and opposite me were Angela and Lisa, looking glassy-eyed.

My mother grabbed a few tacos with the tongs and recounted the scene in the principal's office, making herself out to be even more spectacular than she had been.

"I'm proud of you for standing up for your rights," Angela said to me.

"I don't see how having belief in God and going to Bible Studies is so bad," my dad said.

"I forbid it," my mother said, glaring at him.

Susie kicked me under the table. It was time to establish our alibi for the night. "We're getting a ride to the library after we do the dishes," Susie said.

I held my breath waiting to hear what my mother might say, but to my relief, she didn't react. Susie winked at me.

With nylons and skirts hidden under our jeans and Bible study aids tucked into our purses, we were free to go.

GETAWAY VAN

As the sun dipped low, we hurried down the hill, glancing back to make sure no one was watching.

"I see their van!" Susie squealed, rushing toward the red and white Dodge.

Phil, in the driver's seat, greeted us with a warm, toothy smile. Tina leaned in and squeezed us each with hugs.

She was tan, with kind blue eyes and short, bleached-blonde hair styled into a perfect shag over large, silver hoop earrings. Even in her knee-length skirt and modest Christian attire, she somehow managed to look effortlessly hip. Their two small children, Christian and Kelly, sat obediently in the front row of the van like perfect little dolls, unmoved by the excitement around them.

It was such a relief to be with them.

"Darls, what does your mother think about you being in such a rough school?" Tina asked.

I tried to explain how busy they were, but Tina didn't seem convinced. "They're too busy to see how scared you are?"

Tina and Phil were different from anyone I'd ever met. They prayed before meals and treated each other kindly—a far cry from the tension and arguments at home. Their house was filled with Jehovah's Witness literature: *Awake!* and *The Watchtower* magazines lay casually on tables, and headlines grabbed my attention—"Is There Life After Death?", "How World Conditions Today Are Fulfilling Bible Prophecies," "Are Drugs the Answer?" Curiously, they had no crosses or religious artwork. The Truth felt modern, logical, and clean—unlike any religion I'd ever seen.

Our parents were agnostic and had abandoned the traditional religions of their youth when they left New York, so we had no real options to satisfy our spiritual curiosity. Susie and I were ripe for the picking.

Susie and I became captivated by their energy—something we could only describe as an aura, which we assumed came from their faith. Tina and Phil offered answers. They spoke of a New System—a biblical promise of peace and brotherly love, interpreted by The Watchtower Society. We'd met them while babysitting their kids, but over time, those babysitting sessions had become Bible studies. Their certainty, warmth, and the promise of immortality drew us in.

We climbed to the last row of seats to change out of our getaway clothes. I scraped my leg on something sticking out of a spare tire and felt my nylons run. The van hadn't moved yet.

I peered out the back window, looking to see if there was any activity coming from our house. My heart was racing and my left eye started to twitch. *I'm not cut out for this*

Bonnie and Clyde lifestyle, I thought. I looked over at Susie; she was as relaxed as I was anxious. *How does she keep her cool?*

Once changed, I settled into a seat and took a deep breath for the first time all day.

"It's hard to understand why your mother would stop you from pursuing a moral life when there are so many people living in sin," Phil said.

"I'm sure she'll come around," Tina said. "By the way, Susie told us you got sent to the principal's office."

Phil chimed in. "I called an Elder in the congregation, Brother Long, to seek his guidance. He has a few ideas on how to handle the issues at school."

I blushed. Their attention felt overwhelming but also affirming.

"Darls, you made an important gesture on behalf of Jehovah," Tina offered. "We're really so proud."

"Thank you," I said. "I'm afraid our mother will find out we're lying about tonight. The way she acts, you'd think I was pregnant."

They both laughed, and their approval melted away some of the awfulness of the day.

Finally, the van headed down the hill—away from my disapproving mother and toward Jehovah. We turned into the parking lot of the Kingdom Hall and filed out of the van to mingle with the other worshippers—clean-cut men dressed in jackets and ties and women dressed plainly and modestly. We all headed into a nondescript one-story building with a sign that read *Kingdom Hall of Jehovah's Witnesses*. There was little indication that it was a religious meeting place; it could easily be mistaken for an Elks Lodge. There were no stained-glass windows or cathedral ceilings, no crosses, paintings, statues, or icons of Jesus.

At the door, greeters smiled and welcomed me with "Hello, Sister Darls." I liked being called Sister Darls—it felt like I belonged to a real family.

I spotted Natalie Roland, a pretty girl my age, whom I had just met the week before. She was standing with her two sisters. Natalie's eyes went immediately to the run in my stockings.

The Rolands had blonde hair and looked like they were modeling the newest clothing line from the Macy's Junior catalog. Their clothes were crisp, new, and expensive looking. Their entire family were pillars of the Jehovah's Witness community. Rosalie, Natalie's oldest sister, was a Pioneer, which meant she devoted herself to a minimum of 100 hours each month going door to door and performing other acts of service. I thought they were so lucky to have Jehovah's Witnesses parents who supported them.

I followed behind Tina as she dropped envelopes in the collection boxes—one for tithing (Jehovah's Witnesses were encouraged to donate 10 percent of their income) and another for reporting hours spent witnessing to others and the money collected for literature.

I longed to have something to contribute.

I sat next to Natalie in a row of folding wooden chairs and followed her cues, first reaching for the song book, then standing to sing. Scanning the room, I saw Susie two seats in front of me, next to Rosalie, and Tina a few rows behind me. I locked eyes with Tina, and she smiled.

Brother Long, the senior Elder, stood at the podium and leaned into the microphone. He directed everyone to be seated as he led the congregation in prayer.

"Jehovah God, please help us learn and understand Your plan for us as we praise You and Your teachings and gather to study Your word. We are thankful for Your generous love and in the name of Jesus we pray. Amen."

Jehovah's Witness prayers were not recited from memory; the only requirement was that they must end with "in the name of Jesus" or they wouldn't be heard by God.

"Amen," the congregation chimed in unison.

My heart filled with gratitude and a sense of knowing God.

Brother Long invited three female members of the Congregation to act out a biblical skit. These small demonstrations depicted ways to use specific persuasive techniques for witnessing to non-believers. In this skit, they were using an article from *Awake!* magazine. Brother Long introduced the three "sisters," saying that two were Pioneers and the third was the Householder, a term for a non-witness. The goal was to bring the Householder into the fold.

This terminology was specific to Jehovah's Witnesses, and knowing it made me feel like an insider.

After the skit, the congregation was encouraged to participate in a group discussion about the topic. Phil raised his hand, and an usher passed him the microphone.

"We have two shining examples of serving Jehovah right here in this room," Phil told the congregation. "Sisters Darls and Susie are here with us at the Kingdom Hall, despite their parents' refusal and disapproval. Sister Darls was sent to the school principal today for abstaining from the false worship of the United States flag."

Natalie looked at me. I felt my face burning with pride and embarrassment.

"These young ladies are stellar examples of devotion to Jehovah and the promise of hope for a New System where Satan and his evil are eliminated forever," Phil continued. "Persecution is a sign of the end of times, and we are sitting in its midst with these fine young ladies."

The agony of this day all made sense now: being persecuted for my religious beliefs brought me closer to salvation. It was a good start to my two-year preparation for the upcoming Armageddon. Jehovah's Witnesses expected an imminent Divine War of Armageddon to end the world, cleansing it of evil. It seemed plausible to me: after all, we had recently experienced and survived the 1971 Sylmar Earthquake—6.6 in magnitude.

The year 1975 was identified as the year the world was to end. The ones who chose Jehovah would receive the gift of eternal life in an idyllic paradise. I had a few years to get in spiritual shape! After the meeting, I was rushed by several congregants who congratulated me for my "long suffering," a term that indicated the pious patience necessary for Jehovah's Witnesses to endure the End of Days. Brother Long approached me and introduced himself. He had a huge physical presence, with a large belly that extended past his belted khakis. He asked me to get my sister and meet him in the office at the back of the Hall.

I found Susie flirting with two boys and grabbed her. "The Elder wants to talk to us!"

There were no priests or pastors in Jehovah's Witnesses. Elders were appointed volunteers—spiritual leaders chosen to oversee the congregation. They had to have a spotless moral record. Their job was to supervise the congregation, oversee the distribution of literature, and, perhaps more importantly, administer discipline. Only men could occupy leadership roles in the congregation. Women participated through the skits and were allowed to comment in the discussion.

We followed Brother Long to the back office and were seated in dark red leather chairs at a round table. He asked about our family. As usual, Susie did the talking.

Brother Long picked at his nails, which were surprisingly dirty, but he wore an attentive smile the whole time; clearly, he found Susie charming. When she finished speaking, he gave us a pep talk about the importance of staying away from worldly people and activities.

This expression "worldly" was used frequently and differentiated Jehovah's Witnesses from the rest of the world—the non-believers.

"I plan to become baptized as soon as I possibly can!" I blurted out.

Susie looked at me and nodded. We hadn't talked about this, but it seemed like the logical next step.

Brother Long dropped the pen from his clipboard and struggled to bend over his extended stomach to reach it. When he stood up his face was red. "You're enthusiastic about being Jehovah's Witnesses and we're proud to have you in our congregation," he said, wiping the sweat from his brow.

I walked out of that office feeling like I'd just gotten a stamp of approval from Jesus himself. Susie and I joined our mentors in the parking lot, where they were making plans with a group to go to Du-Pars for pie. Susie told them we could go, but the idea of going home late to our parents—where we might have to face our lies and their consequences—filled me with dread.

Tina saw my expression and nudged Phil. "Let's take the girls home first, just in case."

They dropped us off at the end of our street. Back in our street clothes, we walked up the hill, unsure of the reception we'd get at home.

Our dad was alone in the living room, watching the news on TV, when Susie and I walked in.

"Why didn't you call me for a ride from the library?" he asked.

"It's okay, Dad, we got a ride," I said.

Susie headed back to our bedroom, claiming she needed to do her posture exercises, leaving me alone to face our father. I stood there, wracked with tension.

"What's wrong, honey?" he asked.

"Can I ask you a question?" I plopped down on the sofa and leaned against him. "Do you think Mom will reconsider her decision? Why is she so against us learning about the Bible?"

He shook his head. "She's feeling a lot of pressure right now about the new business. Maybe give it some time."

I started to cry, and my father put his arm around me. I settled into his embrace, remembering when he'd briefly studied Scientology several years earlier. He'd spoken about the teachings enthusiastically, seduced by the hope of self-improvement and immortality. He'd been convinced the answers to life were there. My mother had been vehemently against it and called it a money-making cult based on science fiction. Dad had given up his association with the religion after about six months. My father was gentle, patient, and calm. He lived with the wrath of my mother along with us kids and I often felt bad for him. Still, this interlude gave me hope. *Maybe one day he'll be more open to listening to the message of Jehovah.*

I had far less hope for my mother, but I wouldn't let that derail me. *No matter what she says or does,* I told myself, *I'm not giving up. I vow to do whatever it takes to enter the Kingdom of God.*

As for the rest of my family, I had to show them the way and pray that eventually they would see The Truth.

PLAYING HOOKY

I was frozen in front of my gym locker, staring at the puke-green logo on my Van Nuys Junior High School shirt.

"Jesus freak! Jesus freak!" three girls in my class chanted at me, over and over.

I couldn't get undressed in front of them. *If only Armageddon could get here sooner*, I thought.

Just then, the coach came in and the girls quieted.

I shuffled over to her. "I have a stomachache. Can I go to the nurse's office?"

She glanced at the group of girls eyeing me and nodded.

This was fantastic news, because my next class was homeroom, which meant I could avoid the whole Pledge of Allegiance issue altogether. I practically skipped down the hall to the nurse's office.

She took my temperature. "It looks normal. Do you wanna lie down for a while?"

"Yes, please," I replied gratefully.

Lying on the army cot in the nurse's infirmary, I considered ways to get out of this school. *Why did my parents have to move here?* I asked Jehovah to give me strength and provide me with an answer. Eventually, I fell asleep.

I woke to the sound of the school bell. The nurse looked over at me and offered a faint smile.

"Your sister Angela is coming to get you," she said. "You've been excused to go home."

In the hallway, the girls from gym class spotted me and formed a barrier to prevent me from passing. One girl pressed me against the wall. As a group, they bodied me into a corner and "called me out"—they wanted to fight.

"You ain't just a Jesus freak, you an *ugly* Jesus freak," one of them said, scratching my arm with her fingernails.

The end-of-lunch bell rang, and I used the distraction to break free and run out of the building, frantically scanning the street for Angela in her rusted blue Chevrolet Corvair.

I spotted her—*Jehovah answered my prayer!*—and rushed to the safety of her car.

"What happened?" Angela threw her lit Marlboro cigarette out the window and grabbed my arm to take a closer look. "Do you want me to go after them?"

"Let's just go home," I said. "They're crazy, and it will only make it worse."

"*General Hospital* is starting in a few minutes," she winked as she peeled out into the street.

I never returned to Van Nuys Junior High School after that day. The first week was easy since I had a cold. The next week, I came up with an excuse each day. Two weeks stretched into four. It was odd that my parents let me get away with avoiding school, but then, they were tending to their business: they were in the middle of opening their new modeling school, also known as a Finishing School.

Since Angela was in charge, she and I had a soap opera–watching marathon while my parents busied themselves with work. I felt like Pippi Longstocking, staying home from school without adult supervision. It felt like I was getting away with murder.

I was shocked that the school hadn't yet reported the situation. Every day I waited for the mail, anticipating a letter from the school attendance office. Nothing came. Maybe the school didn't want me as much as I didn't want them.

By the third week of my truancy, Susie had become more and more appalled by my parents' apathy—and angry at the way I had been treated at school.

"Darls, how can Mom and Dad not do anything?" she demanded. "You're being persecuted at school!"

"What are they supposed to do, Susie?" I asked. "I'm going to have to get up the courage to go back and face those mean girls. I've been praying about it."

She shook her head and then suddenly jumped from her seat. "I have an idea!"

She ran to get the phone book and came back with a pen and a pad of paper. We moved to the kitchen counter, where she opened the Yellow Pages, turned to the P's, and found the listing for "private schools." We looked at the ones with the biggest ads first.

"Small classes, individualized attention." Susie jabbed her finger at the ad. "This one."

She scribbled a pitch and prepared to read the script like a seasoned telephone solicitor. Within minutes she was dialing.

"Hello, my name is Susan Centola," she began, confidently. "My younger sister and I are seeking a school that offers scholarships. We're straight-A students and known for our good citizenship. I'm in ninth grade and my sister is in seventh. Can you direct me to the right person to speak with?"

I was impressed by her professionalism. Then again, this was not Susie's first rodeo. Earlier that year, when she'd decided she wanted to learn ballet, she'd finagled a scholarship at a dance studio where she now helped clean in exchange for lessons.

The first call resulted in an immediate "no." I was convinced it would never work—that I was doomed to be beaten up by barbaric teenagers. I felt my stomach tighten, ashamed that we were asking for something for free, like beggars.

"What if we helped clean the school in exchange for a scholarship?" Susie suggested. "Do you mean, be janitors?" I didn't like the idea, but I also didn't think her scheme would amount to anything. "It's worth a try," she said, and I shrugged.

Susie continued her cold calls. She encountered dozens of rejections before finally calling Cal Prep, which had a large advertisement with a coat of arms in the Yellow Pages.

"My name is Susie Centola," my sister began, "and my sister and I would be willing to exchange janitorial services in return for tuition at your school—we can't stand the Van Nuys public schools, and our parents don't have enough money to afford private school." She made her request in one breath.

The woman who answered the phone seemed unfazed by Susie's approach. Her name was Ruth Yardum, and her southern accent was audible. "I'm intrigued and impressed by your boldness," she said to Susie.

In ten minutes, Susie and Ruth Yardum covered the basics. By the time my sister hung up the phone, as unbelievable as it seemed, we'd been accepted to Cal Prep.

CAL PREP

Cal Prep became home for the next four years. In exchange for tuition, Susie and I were expected to complete daily chores, conduct ourselves as model students, and earn good grades. This wasn't a stretch for me—my teachers made a case for me to skip two grades ahead and I did so easily.

Our custodial duties were to empty trash cans, clean the dry-erase boards, and tidy up the bathrooms. It took us about thirty minutes at the end of the school day. I was embarrassed to be dumping plastic bags of trash and wielding toilet bowl scrubbers as our classmates got picked up by chauffeurs, but at least I wasn't at that horrid school anymore.

And there was no morning Pledge of Allegiance.

When we enrolled, Cal Prep was in a house and had fewer than twenty-five students. The only thing that looked school-like about it was the wall of lockers in the mint green, mosaic-tiled kitchen.

But within a few years Mrs. Yardum had purchased a massive triple lot across the street, built an eye-catching, ultra-modern, bright orange and white octagon building, and increased enrollment to several hundred.

Mrs. Yardum was an heiress, an entrepreneur, and a Georgian southern belle who loved Ayn Rand and Ronald Reagan, the governor of California at the time. We shared a passion for literature, and I was drawn to her collection. I told her about my favorite books—I'd read everything by Pearl S. Buck, Louisa May Alcott, Chaim Potok, Mark Twain, Ernest Hemingway, and Jane Austen—and she graciously lent me her own books, one at a time. I quickly devoured each one, anticipating the conversations we'd have about them later.

Mrs. Yardum seemed to enjoy my company—other than the fact that I was a Jehovah's Witness. More than once, she expressed the notion that I would eventually "grow out of" this "cult religion." As a result, I edited myself around her and limited my attempts to convert her.

Eventually my duties grew to working in the school's gift shop, assisting Mrs. Yardum with school administration, and organizing her personal paperwork. She invited me to sit on the other end of the couch in her office to rub her pantyhose-covered feet while she spoke of her adventures in business, European travels, and philosophies on life. Sometimes the stories included dalliances outside of her marriage.

"Women in France are much more liberated when it comes to monogamy, you know," she said one day.

I didn't, but preferred staying on that topic as opposed to hearing more about her low opinion of Jehovah's Witnesses.

"Darls, you're so smart." She shook her head. "How could you believe in such a confining and condemning version of Christianity? You know it's a cult when the thought and belief system is closed and doesn't allow for outside thinking."

I wasn't sure what that meant, but I didn't forget it.

I enjoyed my role as protégé, her secret keeper. Mrs. Yardum alluded to my academic career as a future Ivy Leaguer. I didn't divulge that Jehovah's Witnesses don't go to college, considering Cal Prep was named for its implicit purpose of "preparing" one for college. Higher education was seen by Jehovah's Witnesses as a futile effort toward a worldly future, filled with worldly people and worldly ideas.

Cal Prep was considered progressive for the early '70s, with a designated smoking section, teachers casually addressed by their first names, and a dress code that allowed for free expression through fashion. Last year's "Dresses Only" rule for girls was dropped and it was typical to see students in flared, low-cut, designer bell-bottom jeans, unisex gold platform boots, and Adidas track and leisure suits.

I, meanwhile, wore mostly hand-me-down clothing and couldn't compete with the ongoing fashion show on parade at the school.

One late afternoon while working in the office, I overheard Mrs. Yardum speaking to the principal, Andre.

"We have those four new students starting tomorrow," Mrs. Yardum said. "We need a plan—there's likely to be a fuss over them."

"I intend to greet them and introduce each one of them to their classes," Andre replied. "I've also spoken to their teachers. Apparently, there's already been a rumor going around, so it shouldn't be a huge surprise."

I'd already heard the rumor; this just confirmed it. Even though Cal Prep had a roster filled with celebrities, this was still exciting news: the Jacksons were enrolling.

THE JACKSONS ARRIVE

On their first day at Cal Prep High School, Michael Jackson and his siblings arrived in a nondescript blue-and-white van. I was walking across the school parking lot, having just gotten off the city bus, when I saw it heading toward the school.

One by one, the Jacksons emerged. Marlon, first out of the van, sported a red fedora and a matching, rhinestone-studded jeans-and-jacket ensemble. Randy, wearing a full, perfectly shaped afro, was more casual in jeans, Converse high-tops, and a purple Lakers jersey with a large number 13 and the name "Chamberlain" printed across the back.

La Toya had long curls in tendrils around her face, capped with a yellow cloth hat that matched the yellow pantsuit cinching her tiny waist. Before that moment, I had never even known there *was* a La Toya Jackson—but there she was, with a Gucci bag and the longest eyelashes I'd seen this side of a makeup counter. I was immediately intrigued; I wanted to know more about this extraordinary-looking girl.

Then Michael stepped out of the van. He wore an electric blue button-up collared shirt and matching bell-bottom slacks. I was captivated by his graceful movements. My stomach dropped a little at how cute he was.

I parked myself at a picnic table and started rifling through my bookbag, pretending to look for something so I could continue to discreetly observe them. I had never thought of myself as the starstruck type before, having spotted many movie and TV stars in Los Angeles, but at this moment I was fascinated.

Why did they leave their former private school, and why mid-semester? I wondered. Perhaps because of a strict uniform and short hair policy—or maybe it was just that Cal Prep was closer to their home in Encino—walking distance, in fact.

"They're the only Black kids at school," someone said quietly.

This hadn't occurred to me, and I thought about how that must feel for them.

Andre walked toward the van as they were getting out and greeted each of the Jacksons with a handshake. He spoke with their driver, an older Black man—maybe their father, I thought—and just then the first of two bells rang, indicating five minutes to get to class.

"Let's go, everyone!" the principal shouted. "You know where you should be!"

I headed to my classroom and slid into my seat.

"Did you see that strange hat the girl was wearing?" one student with perfect Farrah Fawcett hair asked me. "I wonder if she's covering something up on her head."

"Like what?" I asked.

Just then the door opened, and La Toya crossed the threshold, escorted by Andre. The class went immediately silent as everyone reached for their books. La Toya had a forced smile on her face and made no eye contact.

"I'll meet you here after class to bring you to second period," Andre said to her, and then left.

All eyes were on La Toya as she stood before the teacher in the front of the class. *It must be agony for her to be on display like this*, I thought. She clutched her oversized purse close to her body with one arm and her white, three-ringed binder with the orange Cal Prep insignia in the other. She was so tiny, she practically disappeared behind them.

Our teacher, Rose—a tall woman with a deep voice and a short haircut—strode over to La Toya.

"You can call me Rose," she said, handing our new classmate a book. "We're three months in, but you'll catch up."

"Thank you, Miss Rose," La Toya said.

"No," Rose corrected her, "we use first names here. Call me Rose."

La Toya's eyes widened. "Okay, Rose," she said softly.

Rose instructed La Toya to sit in a chair close to her. We were reading *Siddhartha* by Herman Hesse, with each of us taking turns covering two paragraphs aloud.

La Toya's turn came in the middle of the first go-round, and her high-pitched voice quivered as she read. The second time she read, Rose barked at her, "Speak up, your voice is too quiet."

I felt bad for La Toya. Her voice was soft, but clear enough to hear.

Between readings, La Toya mostly looked down at her book, blinking her eyes a lot, and for a minute I thought she might be crying. I could see little droplets of glue where her eyelashes were individually applied. Her pink porcelain fingernails were unusually long and curved, with little sunflower decals on the index fingers.

I empathized with La Toya's position as a newcomer and understood the feeling of being an outsider. I'd felt the same way when I started Cal Prep two years prior, arriving late in the semester. I thought about which of the girls in class might become her friend, discounting myself as a contender.

Studying her tiny presence, I compared myself to La Toya and felt like a Goodyear Blimp. The girls at my school looked like celebrities—flawless figures, salon blow-dried hair, Jordache jeans, and 14-carat-gold jewelry. La Toya fit in perfectly with them.

I made sure to smile at her, trying to show her I was an ally. I wanted to tell her how I felt about the way the teacher had treated her and was planning my opening line—but as soon as the bell rang, Andre appeared and walked her to her next class.

In the common area between classes, I saw Michael Jackson being escorted to his second period by another student. I was struck by Michael's gentle gait and how his stylish clothes looked so good on his tall frame and broad shoulders. He reminded me of Fred Astaire with his long, lean dancer's legs. He held his hand over a tortoise shell hair pick in his back pocket; I surmised he used it to tend to his large, flawless afro. I thought he was cuter than any other boy at Cal Prep, except Christian Brando.

When I passed them, the escort wore a proud smile, and we exchanged a knowing look.

Finally, I got to see Michael up close. I noticed he had makeup thickly smeared on his face, unsuccessfully covering acne that looked red and painful. Michael kept his head bowed and held his hands behind his back as he walked past me down the hall. I got the same feeling from him that I had from La Toya: I could sense his uneasiness; there was a fragility about him. His shoulders were tense and hunched toward his ears, like he was protecting himself. Everyone was watching him and some kids smiled at him in passing, but because his head was down, he didn't acknowledge them. It seemed to me that he would have shrunk himself into oblivion, given the option.

At the end of the school day, I met Susie, and we walked to the bus stop together. She said Marlon Jackson was in her math class and Michael was in her art class.

"I think people stared at them too much," she said. "I felt bad. I didn't see very many kids trying to speak with them, so I introduced myself to Michael."

I envied the ease Susie had to strike up a conversation with anyone.

"He was nice, but it seemed like he didn't want to talk much. I asked him some questions about where he went to school before. He's a really good artist—I saw him sketching during the entire class and he barely looked up from his page."

"Did he answer your questions about his other school?" I asked. "His responses were short, one-word answers," she said. 'Montclair' and 'Just a few years.'"

"I think he might be really shy like La Toya, who's in two of my classes," I said.

"I think Marlon is the cutest, but they're all so good-looking," Susie said.

I didn't share that I thought Michael was the most darling. My boy-craziness was starting to become distracting, and I knew I needed to be careful about letting these thoughts intensify.

FAMILY DINNER

After school, our dad was waiting for us at the bottom of the hill in his white 1973 Cadillac.

"How was your day among the rich and famous?" he grinned as we slipped inside.

He loved that we were bucking the system, and he took great pride in our attending an expensive private school on scholarship.

Susie and I exchanged glances but neither of us said anything. I was dying to tell him about the Jacksons, but Susie had made me promise to wait until dinner to share the big news.

That night we sat in our usual seats, with my mother at the head of the table. She'd just come home from the modeling school and was wearing a white silk blouse with pearl buttons covered by her favorite red apron. She was home for the evening meal but would be returning to work soon afterward.

"How wonderful to have you all present this evening," my father said in his typical joking tone.

Our dogs were barking over one another.

"Put those goddamn dogs in the back while we're eating," my mother ordered.

"Juney, is there anything new with the potential investors?" my father asked.

"Frank, you know how I feel about discussing this subject at the dinner table."

I was relieved she shut him down; they'd been fighting a lot about their money problems and struggling new venture lately.

Dad asked us what was new at Cal Prep—and that gave me the permission I needed to finally tell everyone about the Jacksons.

Susie and I shared all the details—their names, which classes we shared, what they were like. Dad seemed genuinely impressed.

"I'm sure Ruth Yardum considers this great publicity for her growing school," my mother said. "Imagine how much money she's going to make in tuition from that family. Maybe you girls won't need to be the janitors anymore."

"We don't even have any Jackson 5 records," Susie said between silent counts. She was on yet another new diet kick where she tried to chew each mouthful of food forty times; supposedly, all that chewing helped with weight loss.

I reached for my second helping and my mom gave me a stern look. "You should take stock in what Susie does with her food intake."

My mother's lack of sensitivity only strengthened my resolve to stay on the path to God, where I felt valued for more than my appearance.

"I think you girls look picture perfect just the way you are," my father said. He was on my side, but he was powerless to stop my mom from all her criticizing. "Juney, think of them as character actors rather than the stars of the show."

Mom glared at him.

Susie took a break from counting to describe what the Jacksons were wearing and how Michael had sketched the entire time he was in class. "He was drawing caricatures," she shared. "He sketched the kids at school all goofy-looking. In one, he drew flies circling the butt of a nerdy, freckle-faced kid with huge glasses."

I envied the intimate view she'd gotten of Michael's sketches. I wondered what other hidden talents he had, and if he and my sister would get closer over the next few weeks.

"I think it'll be tough for them to start the school year so late," Susie said. "How will they catch up with their classes?"

"I overheard a discussion about that in the office," I answered. "When the Jacksons travel, they have a tutor who works with their teachers. It's the law that school-age kids receive educational work at least three hours per day, even if they are in show business and on the road."

"Well," my mother said, "I hope we'll be able to afford the tuition for you and Susie by next year. I'm tired of you girls being a charity case."

This seemed highly unlikely.

LA TOYA

The next day at school, La Toya was placed in another one of my classes, history.

She and I walked into the classroom simultaneously and the teacher pointed at two side-by-side desks; he wanted us to sit by each other. I was happy to have an opportunity to get closer to the mysterious Jackson girl.

"Darls, will you please get La Toya up to speed on how we structure the current events assignment?" the teacher requested.

From then on, we sat next to one another during history class; a week later, we walked together to our nutrition break.

Nutrition was a highly social part of the school day and could be intimidating if you were new. "I'm going to get a cheese Danish and orange juice," I said as we walked down the hall. "Can I get you some? The cheese is the first to go and then there'll only be prune left, so I'm gonna rush."

"No, thank you," she said quietly as we set our books down at one of the round orange picnic tables.

"Be right back," I said, feeling like a fool for talking about pastries.

No wonder she's so tiny and I'm not. She must think I have no self-control.

As I turned to go, I noticed some of the more fashionable girls approaching her. I hoped I hadn't missed my opportunity to spend time alone with her.

Heading back to the table, I saw Kathy Richards talking to La Toya. Her sister, Kim, was in a bunch of popular movies, and Kathy herself was blonde, beautiful, and always well-dressed.

As I approached the table, Kathy turned to me and asked, "Didn't you used to be the janitor at school?"

I felt myself turning red. "Not anymore. Now I work in the office." I'd hoped not to disclose my scholarship status. It was a constant source of embarrassment, and I was afraid La Toya would think less of me.

She turned back to La Toya. "Where did you get that outfit? It's so cute."

"I don't remember," La Toya said dismissively.

I was so happy when Kathy and her friends walked away from our table and La Toya and I were finally alone again.

"My sister and I used to help clean up," I explained, my ears still burning. "We assist with some work in the office and agree to earn good grades and set positive examples in exchange for our tuition."

"That's neat," La Toya said.

I didn't think it was neat, but I was relieved she didn't think it was pathetic.

"I noticed you were dropped off by yourself today," I said. "Are your brothers out of town?"

"The boys had to go to New York," she said, "but they have a tutor who travels with them." She pointed toward a picnic table full of students and teachers, all of them smoking. Kids were bumming drags off each other's cigarettes and blowing smoke rings. "Why are they allowed to smoke? That would *never* be allowed at my old school."

I told her it was a recent development. Many of the smokers had been going off campus, spilling into the neighborhood and disturbing residents and businesses. This was Mrs. Yardum's solution to that problem.

"I know it seems kinda odd," I said, "but Mrs. Yardum's philosophy is to increase attendance and reduce sneaky behaviors by allowing kids to be kids."

As I spoke, my voice was drowned out by the thunder of a loud car engine. We turned to watch a shiny candy-red Ferrari zoom down the school driveway and park in the lot.

John Yardum, Mrs. Yardum's eldest son, climbed out of the car. His wasn't the only Ferrari in what increasingly looked more like a parking lot for movie executives than students.

"Mrs. Yardum's sons used to attend Buckley, but they had too much homework, so she opened her own school," I informed La Toya. As the words came out of my mouth, I realized how crazy that sounded, but she seemed unfazed.

Chucky Starr approached us wearing silver platform boots. With his spiky, bright red hair, he was an androgynous-looking David Bowie clone.

"Love your eyelashes and nail polish," he remarked. "Are your shoes Louis Vuitton?"

La Toya giggled and shook her head as he stood waiting for an invitation to join us. I didn't offer and neither did she, to my relief. Finally, I was getting a real chance to bond with her.

"Do you drive?" she asked as Chucky disappeared into the crowd.

I laughed. "I'm only fourteen."

Her eyes widened. "Wait—you're graduating at fifteen?"

"Yeah, but I'll be sixteen soon," I said quickly, hoping I didn't sound like a little kid."

I'd never known a teenager who wasn't counting the days till they could drive, especially in Los Angeles car culture.

A cute boy and girl walked by us, arm in arm.

"That's Jim and Joy," I said. "They've been together forever. Do you have a boyfriend?" I immediately regretted asking.

"No," she said emphatically. "Never."

I was starting to get the sense that La Toya Jackson was not a typical teenager. In fact, she seemed sheltered from the real world, more innocent than most sixteen-year-olds. We were two years apart, but she seemed more my age.

"Where does your family live?" she asked me.

"In Sherman Oaks. Up Beverly Glen." What I didn't tell her was that we'd just lost our large house on the hill overlooking the Valley and would likely be moving into an apartment *north* of Ventura, on the other side of the tracks.

"That's neat," she said again. Then she turned to look directly at me. "I noticed you carry a Bible around with you. What religion are you?"

I steeled myself and smiled. "I'm a Jehovah's Witness. And so's my sister, Susie."

"Are your parents Jehovah's Witnesses?" she asked with interest. "Do you go to the Kingdom Hall?"

"No one else in our family studies The Truth," I answered. "My sister and I converted a few years ago... How do you know about Jehovah's Witnesses?"

She explained that her mother had become a baptized Jehovah's Witness when they were young kids living in Gary, Indiana. "Mother is devout, but my brothers lost interest as they got older and busier," she said. "But my sister Rebbie lives in Kentucky with her husband, who is an Elder. I've gone to meetings before but not for a while. I wish I were more involved."

Not only did she know about Jehovah's Witnesses, but she wanted to be *more involved*. I was amazed.

From then on, we started going to nutrition together after history class every day. I loved the feeling of walking next to her, enjoying what others might be thinking. It had seemed so unlikely that La Toya would select me as her person, the one she let in, but here I was, the only person she spent time with one on one.

I held my head higher and felt special in her presence.

RECRUITING FOR JEHOVAH

A few weeks later, on the way home from school, Susie delivered some unexpected news.

"Michael Jackson approached me today and asked if I would study the Bible with him."

A flurry of questions flew out of me: "When will you begin? How will you arrange it with his frequent travels? Did you make a plan?"

"Actually, I told him he should ask you because you're more of an avid Bible student," she said casually. "He said he wasn't exactly sure who you were, but when I described you, he said he'd seen you in the office."

"Wow, are you *sure* you don't want to have the Bible study?" I asked. "It'll help you build your hours of service as we get ready to be baptized."

"I'm too busy with dance school right now, and you study more than me," she said.

"But you can do it during the lunch break..." *Wait, why am I arguing with her?* Jehovah heard my prayers. Maybe this would be my chance to have my own Bible student—to be to someone else what Tina was to me. It would be an important steppingstone toward being baptized and becoming a bona fide Jehovah's Witness.

I suddenly felt overwhelmed.

"What should I do, Susie? Is he going to ask me or should I approach him? What do you think? I mean, what if he is too afraid to ask me? I think I need to speak with him directly, and right away. What if he changes his mind?!"

"Don't have a cow over it!" she said, shaking her head.

As soon as we arrived home, I called Tina.

"Hi, it's Darls," I managed to say, catching my breath.

"Darls, is everything okay?" she asked. "Is there an emergency?"

"No—well, actually, yes, there is," I blurted. "I need some advice. Michael Jackson wants to study The Truth with me."

"Darls, you know females are meant to work with other females," she said. "That is how the Witnesses conduct studies."

I felt deflated. *Why didn't I think of that?* "I don't know what to do now," I moaned. "What if he loses interest? He's so shy and so busy. What should I do?"

"Well, lemme think... I'm sure there are exceptions," Tina comforted. "I'll make a call to Brother Long."

I sat by the phone, praying, until Tina called back five minutes later. Brother Long said they could make an exception in this case. I wondered if it was because of Michael's celebrity status.

Whatever the case, I was so relieved I blurted out, "I love you, Tina, and I love you, Jehovah!"

Tina giggled and recommended using the book *The Truth that Leads to Eternal Life*, the one we'd studied together first. "The good news is that it'll be fresh in your mind."

I felt sick to my stomach as I hung up the phone. I didn't want to fail at representing Jehovah. *What if Michael doesn't like me or how I teach?*

Lunch period was almost over when Michael Jackson came looking for me under the tree behind the school. Everybody at Cal Prep knew I spent my lunch hours beneath that weeping willow tree, studying the Bible.

Spending my lunchtime reading the Bible was proof of my commitment. Now, however, with the possibility of Michael Jackson becoming part of my spiritual practice, lunchtime—and my life—was starting to look more exciting.

He was wearing a matching vest-and-bell-bottoms ensemble, accompanied by expensive-looking leather loafers. I pretended not to see him and turned my eyes quickly back to the pages of my open Bible.

He called out to me from a distance: "Hi, I'm Michael!"

Like I don't know that.

His voice was high and soft. As he moved closer, I smelled his cologne. He took a hair pick out of his back pocket, and, poking at his afro, casually said, "I heard you're a Jehovah's Witness. I'm in art class with your sister, Susie, and she told me to speak with you about Bible training. She said you know the scriptures inside and out."

It was as if I'd just left my body. Here was this cute boy, talking to me behind the school, alone—that was enough to make me feel elated, flattered, and self-conscious beyond description. To say nothing of his celebrity.

I managed to maintain my composure. "Yes, I've been studying The Truth for a few years and I'm preparing to get baptized soon."

"That's cool," he said. "I'm real interested in getting more involved. Toya said she's in class with you and that you're different from the other kids. Should we get started right away?"

He seemed nervous, plucking leaves and twigs from the tree, twisting and snapping them. My eyes were drawn to his large, expressive hands and long, slender fingers. They were the most beautiful hands I had ever seen.

I looked up and steadied my gaze. "Yes! Let's begin by studying the book *The Truth that Leads to Eternal Life*." A giggle escaped me after I said this, to my great annoyance. I hoped it didn't make me come across as insincere or lacking confidence.

"That sounds like a great idea!" Michael giggled back.

Well, at least we both giggled after saying things that weren't especially funny.

"I'm going to the Kingdom Hall tonight and can get you a copy," I said quickly. "Do you have a Bible? It might be good to use the version that accompanies the book. It's the New World Translation and it's more authentic than other versions of the Bible because it relies on the original Hebrew and Greek sources. Plus, it uses modern language." I felt very smart for knowing not only the name of the translation but also its background.

"Oh, I know which one you mean," he said. "It has a brown leather cover and gold lettering and a little ribbon as a placeholder, right? My mother has that one, but I probably need one of my own."

"That's right," I said, nodding. "I'll get you one of those tonight."

A rush of gratitude spread across his face, illuminating his smile and big brown eyes—filling me with a sensation that my life had just changed. I'd been sought out by someone in search of the same things I was.

Just like that, my isolation was over.

A flurry of questions streamed out of me: "Should we begin tomorrow? What do you think about using the lunch break as our study hour? I notice you go home for lunch—would it be okay to stay here one day per week?" I immediately regretted mentioning him going home for lunch; I didn't want him to know I'd been watching him.

But he seemed unbothered, and he surprised me with his next question: "Can we meet more than once a week? I leave town so often, and I really want to make some progress."

My Bible study with Tina was only once a week and I wasn't sure if this was proper protocol—but I figured I'd sort it out later. I nodded my agreement.

Michael reached up to grab another small branch from the tree and I spotted a dark patch of sweat on his shirt under his arm. As he held the twigs in his fingers, I noticed he was shaking a little, the same thing that happened to me when I had to speak in front of a group. I wondered why; I couldn't imagine that conversing with me was anxiety-provoking for him. After all, this was someone who sang to live audiences of thousands of people, not to mention millions on television.

"Would it be okay with you if we went off campus somewhere to do our study?" he asked. "I really don't want to be interrupted or have people in my business."

"Yes, that's a great idea!" I said eagerly. "I know of a little spot behind the school. We can meet here under the tree when the lunch bell rings and head out. I'll have your books tomorrow."

The end-of-lunch bell rang, and I was sort of paralyzed. I didn't want to assume we would walk back to class together, but Michael started walking, then turned around and said, "C'mon."

He seemed to stiffen as we made our way to the main school building. He moved with caution, careful to walk at a distance from other kids, his head lowered. He kept to his own lane, and I was in it with him. I noticed many students eagle-eyeing us and whispering to one another.

No matter what they were saying about me, it was okay. Others might see me as a geek, but I was the one who was walking side by side with Michael Jackson.

FIRST BIBLE STUDY

While riding the bus to school the following day, I held Michael's copy of *The Truth that Leads to Eternal Life* and said a quiet prayer to Jehovah, asking for His help as I prepared to lead my very first Bible study.

When I saw La Toya in English class, she immediately relieved my worries about studying with her brother.

"Michael told me you're meeting at lunch to read a Bible study book together." She offered me a smile. "I think that's so great. I know he's looking forward to it."

Yes! I had been hoping for her approval and that this might be the start of us all being friends.

I had everything ready: My copy of the book, which was dog-eared and underlined with lots of notes written in the margins. Two copies of *New World Translation Bible*, mine and one for Michael. Plus, two pens, two highlighters, and two notebooks. All were wrapped up neatly in a red canvas tote bag.

The lunch bell rang, and I hurried to the back of the school. Michael was already there under the willow tree, wearing another sharp outfit. He spotted me and smiled. I felt a warmth wash over me.

I greeted him, then beckoned him forward. "C'mon, let's go."

We walked out the back driveway of the school property and went to a concrete storm drain overhung by eucalyptus trees.

I used my arm to hold back some of the brush and pointed behind it. "Do you think you'll be comfortable here? We can sit on the ledge. It's like a bench. I come here sometimes when I need peace and quiet."

Michael looked around and smiled. "Wow, I never knew this was here. It's so private, and it smells so good! I saw some koala bears in Australia eating eucalyptus leaves when I was there. I think the leaves might be poisonous to humans, but only if you eat them." He picked up a handful of leaves and inhaled, then put them in front of me to take a whiff.

I had never connected the storm drain's aroma with leaves from the eucalyptus trees that blanketed Southern California. I was the teacher, but here he was, already enlightening me.

I also noticed how much more relaxed his demeanor was in our hidden place. He took another deep breath of the menthol-scented leaves, then looked up and pointed out a squirrel in the tree.

"Let's call him Preppy," he suggested, laughing. But this laugh was different from the self-conscious giggles of our first conversation. It seemed to come from an authentic place of deep-down joy—and it was contagious.

I laughed, too, in a way much heartier than my usual awkward giggle.

I pulled out my arsenal of study materials, but we never got beyond the book cover. Each time I opened the table of contents, Michael asked me another question. He was curious about the frequency of my attendance at the Kingdom Hall, how long I'd been studying, and what had gotten me involved. Echoing what La Toya had shared with me, he told me his mother had been a Jehovah's Witness before their move to Los Angeles and his eldest sister, Rebbie, was one as well. He said he was ready to get more involved.

"Look at the way the world is today, Michael," I said. "It's filled with misery and human suffering. Imagine an earth filled with only harmony and tranquility—no murder or hatred, no illness or death, just eternal life among the animals, where the lion will lie with the lamb in a garden setting. It's Jehovah's promise of paradise on earth."

He nodded, his eyes shining. He seemed as enamored of the idea as I was.

As we headed back to campus, Chucky Starr sauntered by in a silver spaceman jumpsuit with matching, shimmering platform boots. He almost looked like he was walking on stilts.

"I'm surprised he doesn't fall off his boots and crack his skull on the asphalt," I said to Michael in a low voice.

"He's probably a frustrated performer and needs to express himself," he responded.

His comment took me by surprise. I was learning how different he was from most kids. I hoped I hadn't disappointed him by taking a dig at Chucky. I admired his empathic perspective and thought he might be an old soul. My mother had gone to several psychics over the years and been told more than once that her fourth born—me—was an old soul. I determined this meant a person who was spiritual and wise beyond their years. I liked thinking that Michael and I might share this special status.

"Let's meet again tomorrow," he said.

I felt like I was floating and was sure this was what it was like to walk on water. I wondered if the biblical reference was about this feeling, which seemed to come from being in service to God.

Michael and I had a Bible study together every day for the rest of the week and all the next week. It was a Jehovah's Witness immersion program for Michael; he was so eager, and his enthusiasm fed my own.

At the end of that second week, Michael said he and his family were going away for a month and he didn't want to lose our momentum.

"Do you think we can do a Bible study through the mail?" he asked.

"Sure," I said, not really knowing how it would work. "I'll give you my new address, because I'm moving soon."

"Okay," he agreed. "Just let me know where to send my letter."

My heart sped up in my chest. I planned to camp out on the sidewalk of my new home and wait for the mail.

THE TRUTH THAT LEADS TO ETERNAL LIFE

Having lost the big house in the hills, we moved into a three-bedroom apartment north of Ventura Boulevard.

Well, some of us did.

With my parents now separated and Angela and Lisa old enough to live on their own, my older sisters moved into their own apartment in Hollywood, while Susie, Mikey, and I moved into the three-bedroom with our mother. My father got his own tiny apartment nearby.

For the first time ever, our family was living apart. My parents' modeling business had ended in bankruptcy, and my mother's drinking intensified.

I had never lived in an apartment before and found it strange—mostly because my father wasn't living with us, although he used any excuse he could find to come over. I shared a room with Susie again, and Mikey had his own room. Having so little space and no yard was foreign to us, but there was an upside: My mother gave up her resistance to us going to the Kingdom Hall.

"I know you think I was born yesterday," she announced at our first dinner in the new apartment, "but I suspect you've been sneaking around my back, participating in those Jehovah's Witness activities."

I spun the wooden lazy Susan in the middle of the table. Lazy Susans were for large families and now we were a relatively small family, just the four of us. "I feel that you're old enough and wise enough to make your choice," my mother continued. "I know in my heart you'll eventually give up this nonsense, because you have a solid foundation to protect you."

"Thank you," Susie said. "We promise to use our best judgment."

That seemed to satisfy my mother. I'd had no idea she was onto us before this conversation, but her life hadn't been easy lately. I didn't know whom I felt sorrier for—her or my dad. They both seemed so lost. I felt grateful that I had The Truth.

I wasn't expecting Michael to stick with the idea of doing a Bible study through the mail, given his busy performance schedule, but I came home from school one day and found not one but *two* letters from him on my bed.

Out of my mind with excitement, I carefully opened an ivory-colored envelope and read his handwritten letter on MGM letterhead.

"Darles," he started (he always spelled my name with an added "e"). "I am here, my letter is late because I've been busy. Write me first to begin the study."

I immediately went to work crafting a thoughtful Bible study. I organized it according to the topic we were covering in the book. I indicated certain passages and then wrote a few questions.

The next day, I asked my father to send it on his trip to the post office.

"What is this, a love letter?" he teased.

I shook my head, but it *was* a love letter of sorts; I had poured my heart into every stroke of my pen, wanting to be a good example for Jehovah and for Michael.

Once Michael was back in town, we studied almost every day in the cool shade of our secret spot.

I took my role as his Bible teacher seriously. I reported our hours of study on a form that I turned in monthly at the Kingdom Hall; to be accurate, I recorded my time, down to fifteen-minute increments, in the margins of my journals. I wholeheartedly believed in this process of indoctrination practiced by Jehovah's Witnesses to convert new members, who in turn would pass the message on to others. But I couldn't deny I was also deeply enjoying spending time with Michael.

Reading passages from the Book of Revelation, we decoded its encrypted metaphors and symbolism—going back and forth, interpreting enigmatic messages, relying on our study guides. For example, according to our guides, the beast with seven heads and ten horns referred to in the Book of Revelation as the "abomination of abominations" represented the United Nations, while "Babylon the Great, the mother of harlots" was the Roman Catholic Church.

This information came from *Aid to Bible Understanding*, written by Ray Franz, who was a member of the governing body of Jehovah's Witnesses at the time. The text was a manic outpouring of detailed and specific interpretations of thousands of biblical references.

Michael insisted that we pray out loud together each day before beginning our study. This was not something I had learned from my own Bible mentor, but it became our ritual. We took turns with the opening prayer.

I often thought about things I could say, wanting to come up with something impressive and clever that would demonstrate my deep devotion to Jehovah. Michael, in contrast, didn't seem to struggle with the flow of his prayers. He spoke to God with a familiar intimacy. He always began with, "Dear Jehovah, the savior of our souls," and always included the neglected animals and needy children on the planet.

"Darls, if you could do one thing to change the world, what would it be?" Michael was adept at asking meaningful questions.

"I'd open an orphanage," I replied without hesitation.

"D, that has always been my vision," he replied, full of excitement. "To build an orphanage on a huge piece of land and use animals as a way to help the children heal."

It was astounding to me that we shared the same vision and compassion for orphans, and I loved that he had started calling me "D."

"What inspired you to want to open an orphanage?" I asked him.

"It's all the traveling we've done," he said. "I've seen so much poverty, and I love to visit orphanages when we go to foreign countries." He beamed. "But really, D, what a coincidence! I can't believe I met someone with the same dream as me."

I've found my soulmate in Michael Jackson, I thought.

"Do you ever feel sad about having The Truth while the rest of your family doesn't?" he asked me.

According to the end-of-the-world theory established by the Jehovah's Witnesses, our non-believing family members would one day perish under the wrath of an angry Jehovah bent on cleansing the earth of evil. Susie and I continued to struggle with the concept of surviving Armageddon without our family. Michael and La Toya faced the same set of consequences, but at least their mother was a believer too.

"Yeah, I do think about it, a lot," I admitted. "But I know if we have hope in our hearts and we pray for them to hear the message, there's a chance for them to make it."

Michael nodded. "But when you describe how opposed your mother is to the religion and I think about Josep's anger and hatred toward The Truth, I'm afraid they'll never understand."

It had taken me a while to become accustomed to him referring to his father by his first name, as well as his pronunciation: He said the "ph" at the end with the sound of a "p" instead of an "f"—as in "Josep."

I knew that Joseph's temper was an issue. Michael often alluded to it with comments like, "Oh no, Josep will be so upset if Marlon's after-school basketball meeting makes us late for rehearsal" or "Josep was in a state last night," but then he'd lighten the serious tone by making a silly face or singing a Bible verse.

I understood the implications of a relationship filled with fear—the ongoing vigilance that came from living with the unpredictability of a rage-filled parent. As I watched my own family disintegrate, this newly shared bond with Michael was like a balm on my own emotional wounds. We both found it confounding that our parents could be so resistant to what we recognized as the only answer to life's big questions. I found it comforting to know that Michael and I shared the same obstacle.

Having moved our books to the top of the concrete wall, Michael was now sketching furiously on a piece of lined paper. The drawing was intricate and featured little beds with toy chests beside them, each brimming over with stuffed animals, dolls, and toys.

"If Armageddon is going to happen next year, in 1975, and every person on earth has the chance to choose Jehovah or perish, what do you think will happen to the orphans of the world?" he asked me.

I had the answer for this one, because I'd raised the same question before: "We trust in Jehovah with all our faith. He knows the heart of every man, woman, and child."

We were quiet for a long moment after I said this, both of us processing the idea.

The next day, Michael and I planned to go out to lunch. I was concerned about money, knowing that I only had a five-dollar budget. I figured that if I ordered a side salad, I should have enough.

Hamburger Hamlet was a few blocks from school, on the bottom floor of a tall office building with mostly adult clientele. Michael asked the hostess for "one of those tables," pointing toward the back of the restaurant. Eyes turned as we were seated.

Sliding into our booth, Michael made a point to sit facing away from onlookers as much as possible.

Almost immediately, a lady approached the table and asked him for his autograph. Michael responded politely, smiling and quickly signing her piece of paper. His shyness faded during the autograph signing; there seemed to be a distinct separation between his show business identity and his personal one. The autograph-seeker asked if I was his girlfriend and Michael simply said, "This is Darls."

After the woman walked away, I studied Michael's face. "Are you bothered by the attention?" I asked.

He shrugged. "I don't know any other way—this is my life," he said. "I'm sorry for the interruption, though."

Michael covered his face with the oversize menu, peering at me from behind it, hiding the big red blemishes on his right cheek. Each time the waiter approached the table, Michael's hand automatically found its way to his face, his palm cupping his chin and his long fingers covering the blotches of broken skin.

I felt flattered that he hadn't denied my status as a girlfriend to the autograph-seeker. By now I had a serious crush on him, although I couldn't admit it to myself. Jehovah's Witnesses considered it wrong to allow the desires of the flesh to grow; they were temptations of Satan and must be fought. Besides, I was his teacher, his Bible mentor. It was wrong for me to have any other intentions.

"I think I'll get the chili," he said, still shielding his face with the menu. "What are you getting, D?"

"I'm not that hungry," I lied. "Maybe just a side salad."

Michael lived in an entirely different universe than the one we shared. He was famous and belonged to the world—constantly meeting new people and loved by millions of fans—and here I was, sitting with him alone, getting his undivided attention.

Our waiter was a tall Black man and Michael addressed him with a familiar tone. After he took our order, I asked how they knew one another and was surprised when Michael said he didn't know him. Michael explained to me that the acknowledgment came from a mutual understanding of a shared heritage.

"It represents solidarity," he added. "Darls, do you notice that other than the waiter, I'm the only Black person in here?"

I hadn't noticed. I wanted to say it was the same at Cal Prep but hesitated, wary of saying anything insensitive or offensive.

"I wonder if that lady thought we were a couple?" His brow crinkled. "Maybe others are thinking we're in a mixed relationship."

I felt a heat wave course through me, and I wiped the resulting perspiration from my upper lip. I'd never heard that expression, "mixed relationship," before—especially in such a personal context.

"Did you know that in some states it would be against the law for a Black and White person to be married?" Michael asked me. "You could get arrested and go to jail."

He told me he'd been collecting books about Martin Luther King and Malcolm X. My parents raised us to respect and value people from all backgrounds. They had no tolerance for "man's inhumanity to man," as my mother referred to the Holocaust, American slavery, and the slaughter of Native Americans. But Michael was coming from another perspective. For him, it was more about the history and current politics of the Black Experience. He spoke with conviction about this subject, with his back straight and head held high—a more confident Michael than I'd previously seen.

"Let's look at the assassination of Martin Luther King, only six years ago in 1968," Michael said, his voice full of passion. He told me that King's murder was a conspiracy, using his knife to make illustrations in the crisp, golden tablecloth.

Once again, I was struck by how much he was giving to *me* when I was meant to be *his* mentor. There was so much of Michael that was unseen—like those metaphors about icebergs being only one-third exposed or the root systems of trees going as deep as the branches are tall.

When the check came, he offered to pay for me. I didn't want to take advantage and insisted on paying for myself.

Walking back to school together, Michael and I dropped the serious lunch conversation and, at his suggestion, fell into a game.

"Guess what was here before this building was built—let's say 100 years ago," he prompted.

I guessed the lot used to be a local saloon for cowboys just before they headed out of town, and that where we were sitting was the spot where they'd tied up their horses. We passed a dry cleaner storefront and Michael said that was where they'd put new horseshoes on the horses before their long journey and that the man who'd owned the shop had a humpback. "They called him Humpback Encino Jack," he quipped.

We laughed and built on that shtick the entire walk back to Cal Prep.

As we approached the school entrance, Michael said, "D, do you think it would be all right if we talked on the phone sometimes about our Bible studies?"

That was more than all right with me. I wrote my phone number on the receipt from Hamburger Hamlet and hoped he didn't notice my hand was shaking just a little.

Maybe he liked me more than I thought. *And maybe I can count the time we spent at the restaurant toward my service hours, since we were discussing the Bible.*

I was pretty sure it counted toward my salvation.

The phone rang around 8:00 p.m. that night; I ran from the bathroom to the living room and quickly lifted the receiver.

"Hello, Centola residence," I said.

"Hi, is Darls home?"

"Hi, Michael. It's me." My stomach did a somersault and I felt winded, just as much from excitement as from the running.

"Hi, D. I had so much fun today at lunch. Let's do that more often. And I have some good news..."

I perked up. "What's the good news?"

"Mother said La Toya and I can start going to your Kingdom Hall. Mother said since I'm studying with you, we should be more connected to the Kingdom Hall. I think she was encouraged by you going even though your parents aren't Jehovah's Witnesses."

This was more than good news. I felt victorious. This was perfect timing regarding my next step, baptism, which required a promise to bring new recruits to Jehovah.

"Michael, this is amazing," I gushed. "Let me know when!"

"We should go for another walk during lunch tomorrow and talk about our Bible studies like we did today," he said. "We can pick a passage and then discuss it."

I said yes, of course; I would have said yes to anything he asked.

HEATHEN WEED

In the mid-1970s, the San Fernando Valley was still a suburban work in progress; much of the natural beauty that Michael and I encountered on our walks was scattered across a hodgepodge of vacant lots. As we trekked through the mud and dust of these uninhabited parcels of land, we approached it as someplace beautiful and magical, as though we were entering the edge of the Amazon jungle. Michael marveled at the myriad shades of green and other colors among the trees and leaves; God, he said, knew no limits, and His creativity was endless.

As we set out on our walk and Bible study one warm, sunny day, Michael suddenly looked down and said, "What's this?"

He bent over and picked the item up. He gasped and turned it over repeatedly for closer examination. "Do you know what this is?" he asked.

I suspected it was a joint—or, more accurately, a roach: the butt end of a smoked marijuana cigarette.

He sniffed it, turned it over in his hands a few times more, and exclaimed, "It's marijuana!"

Since he was in the world of rock and roll, I assumed he'd been exposed to all kinds of drugs, especially pot. I personally knew lots of people who smoked pot, including my mother and sisters.

"Do you think it was one of the kids from school?" Michael asked. "I wonder what other drugs they're using. This is the work of Satan, don't you think?"

I agreed with him. I couldn't confess I had tried my sister's marijuana before becoming a Jehovah's Witness. If he knew I had a history with it, I feared he wouldn't want me as a friend or a Bible mentor anymore.

Just then, two big dogs appeared from behind a broken fence and started coming after us. Michael took off and I ran alongside, trying to keep up. I fell behind and Michael grabbed my hand. We ran side by side for nearly a half a mile, through weeds and patches of mud and dirt, holding hands the whole way. After we stopped running, our hands stayed connected for another thirty seconds.

I certainly wasn't going to let go first.

It was Michael who let go, although not until we got back to our secret alley and tried to compose ourselves. He bent down to look at his shoes, which were caked with dirt, then flung them off his feet and proceeded to clean them with a giant leaf.

We caught our breath for a minute. Michael sat down and picked up the study book. As he looked down into it, I could see his shoulders jiggling—he was trying to hide his laughter. "Oh, D, you should've seen your face, you looked so scared!"

Again, I wondered if he liked me more than a friend. I knew I needed to refrain from desirous thoughts, but I couldn't stop thinking about the warm feeling of holding his hand. Our strict doctrine prohibited dating unless it led to marriage; sex before marriage was referred to as "fornication." Boy/girl attractions were much too immoral to even entertain privately, much less admit out loud. To even entertain my feelings felt like I was going to die a sinful death in Armageddon.

BAPTISM

Getting baptized as a Jehovah's Witness was a sacred ritual, but I was so concerned with my appearance in a bathing suit that I couldn't focus on the spiritual aspect of the important event. Susie and I were taking the plunge together, and it didn't help that she was supermodel material. I was disappointed in myself for being so self-conscious. I wanted to set a good example for Michael, who had started regularly coming to the Kingdom Hall with La Toya and their mother, Katherine. They looked up to me—and here I was, obsessing about my thighs. I felt like a failure.

Getting baptized was a three-pronged process. First, the candidate must demonstrate knowledge of God through daily Bible study and regular attendance at the Kingdom Hall—*check*. I knew I was perceived as studious by my mentors. Second, the person must be of a responsible age (no infant baptisms), because they must be able to not only hear and embrace the word of God but also decide to dedicate their lives to God—*check*. I was fourteen and soon to be fifteen. The third step was a total commitment to teaching others and spreading the word of God by creating disciples like the early Christians did, door to door with members of the congregation—*check*. Michael was my Bible student and I reported hours of service by submitting them to the count kept by the Watchtower Society.

Approval for baptism also meant freedom from sexual immorality, smoking, drug abuse, and other sinful behavior. I felt sure that I qualified, even though I had the tiny marijuana infraction from my past. And there was no sexual immorality on my part, except for one incident: When I was twelve, not long before I became a Jehovah's Witness, my uncle—an ex-convict and supposedly recovered junkie—had sexually assaulted me.

I had never talked about what Uncle Kenny did to me, not with Tina nor anyone else. It was unspeakable; I'd buried it somewhere deep. The preparation for the baptism had awakened the memory in an unexpected way. I knew, at least logically, that I wasn't to blame. But part of me felt responsible—after all, my uncle had told me it was *my* fault. If I didn't speak of it, I thought, I could create the illusion of eradicating it. And baptism was the ultimate spiritual cleanse; it would wash away the disgrace forever.

I told Michael and La Toya about the approaching Assembly at the new location, even though I was secretly wishing they wouldn't attend. As it turned out, they were going out of town for a few weeks and couldn't make it. I felt guilty for being relieved.

I agonized over the bathing suit and ultimately borrowed one from Angela, who was twice my size. I barely filled the breast cups, and the faded suit had a little tear in the stomach. We wore white T-shirts and shorts over our bathing suits, but knowing that didn't make me much more comfortable. Tina recommended I wear a robe right up to the edge of the baptismal pool and grab it immediately after to keep from experiencing prolonged discomfort.

Natalie was there that day, looking like a *Teen* magazine cover model with her perfect figure and cute bathing suit. In the dressing room while we were getting ready for the baptism, she looked me up and down and asked, "Is that your mother's suit?"

I mumbled something unintelligible, shrinking from her critical gaze.

During the ceremony, I did as Tina had suggested and looked at her for comfort while I walked to the sacred ritual. She smiled at me from among the onlookers and her shining blue eyes gave me courage. I'd been told to pray intensely before this moment, as I was about to dedicate my life to Jehovah, but my mind was so scattered that I couldn't focus on a cohesive prayer. I consoled myself with the knowledge that Jehovah knew my heart and if I were *trying* to pray, He would lovingly accept it.

I took the long walk toward the pool, flung off the robe, and stepped in quickly. The warm water came up to my shoulders. Brother Long was in the middle of the pool wearing a white T-shirt.

"Have you repented of your sins and turned around, recognizing yourself before Jehovah God, as a condemned sinner who needs salvation, and have you acknowledged to Him that this salvation proceeds from Him, the Father, through his Son Jesus Christ?" he asked me.

"Yes," I answered wholeheartedly, relieved my thighs were submerged in the water.

"On the basis of this faith in God and in His provision for salvation, have you dedicated yourself unreservedly to God to do His will henceforth, as He reveals it to you through Jesus Christ and through the Bible under the enlightening power of the Holy Spirit?" he asked.

Again, I said, "Yes."

His two questions answered, Brother Long told me to hold my nose and then dipped me backwards, submerging my head and shoulders. When I came up, the large cups of the suit flooded with water and the weight almost bared my breasts under my see-through T-shirt. I grabbed the top of the suit and held it in place.

Now cleansed of my sins and devoted to Jehovah, I felt renewed. I was so overcome that I could barely hear the clapping as I climbed the steps and grabbed my robe. Tina, Phil, and Susie were there to hug me.

I sat in the auditorium afterwards and took stock of this new life—my supporters, Tina and Phil, whom I considered my chosen family; hundreds of brothers and sisters, like-minded disciples of Jehovah; and my role as a Bible mentor to Michael. How far I'd come.

Susie and I went to Monty's Steakhouse for a celebration meal with the Rolands. The conversation turned to the events of the day and recognition that we were now representatives of Jehovah, with the responsibility to bring new members into The Truth.

"Just because you're baptized, remember that doesn't guarantee a place in God's New Order," Rosalie announced. "You'll be judged based on the merits of your latest deeds."

Natalie ignored her sister's morbid warning and brought up a magazine article she'd read that outlined a feud between Donny Osmond and Michael Jackson. Of course, she looked at me and raised her eyebrows, as if posing a question.

Standing firm in my loyalty to Michael, I said, "I don't think that article is based on facts."

Michael and La Toya seemed so much more spiritual to me than the Rolands. The Jacksons were far more down-to-earth than my Jehovah's Witness friends. I would count the days until they came back to Los Angeles.

SOUL TRAIN

Michael called me on a Friday. They'd just returned home, and he asked if I could save seats for the three of them for Sunday's meeting at the Kingdom Hall.

"Yes, absolutely!" I said.

Michael told me he'd been thinking about our dream to open an orphanage and had a burning question. I was flattered to be the one he sought out for answers, especially with my new status as a baptized Jehovah's Witness, but also uncertain I would have the correct response.

"If every person on the planet, around 2.5 billion, must hear the message of Jehovah and accept it or refuse," he posed, "what about those who've already passed away—like my grandfather, who never accepted Jehovah into his heart?"

This was a good question; I'd often pondered this same dilemma. In our last study we had covered Matthew 24:14: *And this good news of the kingdom will be preached in all the inhabited earth for a witness to all the nations; and then the end will come.* This was interpreted to mean that every inhabitant on the planet would have a chance to accept or reject Jehovah, but it didn't cover those who had passed away.

"I'm not sure," I admitted. "But maybe Tina knows."

When Tina picked me up to babysit the next day, I repeated Michael's question.

"God grants Jesus the power to raise the dead," she told me. "As written in John 11:25, Jesus will restore all those in the memorial tombs to life, each one with his unique identity, personality, and memories."

"Okay, I'll let him know," I said, then added that the Jacksons would be attending Kingdom Hall the next day.

I beamed at her and Tina beamed back. I'd made her proud.

The next day I watched Michael on TV. He was on *Soul Train*, which aired every Saturday. I had seen a commercial advertising his upcoming appearance and felt like a voyeur—I'd never have watched the show if I didn't know him. At the same time, I felt the pride of being an insider; I knew that Michael dreaded those performances because it meant he had to work on the weekend. He'd just come back to town from a heavy-duty two-week performance tour, and now he had to go back to work.

I no longer saw his constant travel as glamorous. He was putting in serious hours of work while the rest of us got to be kids and simply attend school.

During his brief interview with the show's flashy host, Don Cornelius, Michael awkwardly responded to each question. My shoulders involuntarily tensed as I vicariously held his struggle in my body. When he sang, though, the public Michael appeared—the Michael Jackson the world knew: confident and masterfully embodying his music. It was weird to watch this version of him. I felt like Natalie with her crush on Donny Osmond.

You're his Bible mentor, I reminded myself, *and you have a duty to represent Jehovah!*

But, oh man, he looked so cute—and I melted at the sight of the beauty mark on the left side of his face.

He called me on Saturday night—two nights in a row! I told him I had an answer to his question. I explained about the resurrection and the scripture Tina had quoted to back up the belief. We spoke enthusiastically about the dead rising from the earth and Michael said he was excited about meeting legends such as Martin Luther King and Henry the VIII. I was impressed by his choices.

He asked about my weekend and then I asked about his. He said he'd had to go straight to the studio to film *Soul Train* and he was tired.

"I happened to see the show and I really liked the song you sang, 'If I Don't Love You This Way,'" I told him. "Michael, you seem so sincere when you're singing, like it's your personal experience." I was like every other teenager in the world, secretly hoping he was directing the song's message to me. "Do you mean the words in your songs while you're singing them? In other words, what I'm trying to ask . . ." I stammered, knowing he hated being interrogated about show business. "Do you ... connect with a feeling that is the same as the meaning of the lyrics?"

He paused before answering. His voice changed and I detected the professional musician taking over. He began to answer with what seemed like a canned response.

"I use a real experience to call up a state of emotion, like thinking about an animal that needs rescuing or a child with an illness," he said matter-of-factly.

I'd hoped for a more satisfying answer.

"I don't really think too much about them—the words, that is," he added. "I'm more focused on the combination of my movement and the music cues."

I supposed that was natural, considering he'd been singing meaningful love songs since he was a small child.

On Sunday, I sat with the Jacksons at the Kingdom Hall and introduced them to several Brothers and Sisters. Katherine was so pretty and soft-spoken, like Michael and La Toya. She hugged me as if we were old friends and said, "Thank you for being a friend to my kids—it means so much to them. My daughter Rebbie is in The Truth. She lives in Kentucky, and I have my roots in this religion. I'm so happy to be here."

I sat between Michael and La Toya, and they followed my cues for standing, sitting, and joining in the singing. I was curious to see how Michael would handle the singing portion and if he'd blend in or stand out. We sang "Just Around the Corner." It was about enduring until the End of Times:

You can hear the songbirds singing,
And you watch the clouds roll by.
Then you're walking in the valley
As the sun shines in a clear blue sky.
You're welcoming your loved ones,
And you can't believe your eyes.
Yes, this earthly Paradise
Was just around the corner...

Michael chose to blend in, singing in a measured volume, not overpowering anyone. I felt eyes burning a hole in my back; when I turned around, I caught Natalie ogling us. I liked that for once she wanted something I had—a relationship with Michael and La Toya Jackson.

"God is love and the one who remains in love remains in union with God and God remains in union with him," Brother Long boomed from the front of the room. "There is no fear in love, but perfect love casts fear out, because fear restrains us. Indeed, the one who is fearful has not been made perfect in love. We love because He first loved us."

Michael leaned into me and whispered, "This is why we're here, showing our love and devotion to Jehovah."

The verse was spiritually uplifting, and we were in sync, intoxicated by the poetry of scripture, the euphoria of being right with God. Michael tapped his feet, and his long fingers moved along the spine of his Bible as we followed the reading. I smiled at him, but Katherine gave him a stern look.

"Stop your fidgeting," she whispered.

Michael smiled at his mother and sat still for a bit; then involuntarily started tapping what seemed to be a song.

I asked him about that later and he said he was composing a melody in his head about the idea that God is love. Michael looked me straight in the eyes and said, "Thank you for bringing me to The Truth, Darls."

At the end of the meeting, Brother Long announced some mundane business, then his tone grew solemn. Reading from a piece of paper, he announced sternly, "Ken Lewis has been disfellowshipped for conduct unbecoming a Christian."

Typically, "conduct unbecoming a Christian" meant fornication. I knew about disfellowshipping, but this was the first time I'd been present for an announcement of one. It seemed like a death had occurred; the atmosphere in the Kingdom Hall grew gloomy and heavy. Getting disfellowshipped was reserved for baptized Jehovah's Witnesses who'd committed a sin that conflicted with doctrine. They were publicly excommunicated by the entire congregation, and shunned by their family. We were all forbidden to have anything to do with them.

Ken was a little older than Susie, who had a big crush on him. He was tall, with dark, curly hair and big freckles. I looked around and saw his mother, father, and brother a few rows away. They looked so distressed. I wondered how they would handle things at home when they weren't allowed to speak or show love to their family member.

As the shock wore off, I had a terrifying thought: Now that Susie and I were baptized, it meant we were held to a higher standard, which also meant we could be disfellowshipped. *Could I be disfellowshipped for my romantic longing toward Michael?* Having a crush is not the same as fornicating, but it *was* wrong.

I wondered what Ken had done and how the Elders had found out. When it came to questionable behavior among family members, Jehovah's Witnesses didn't see it as a private matter; they viewed secrets they discovered about other Witnesses as a gift from God. In other words, people were encouraged to tell on family members who might be misbehaving. I felt so afraid for Ken; we were heading into 1975 and Armageddon.

After the meeting, we were swarmed by congregation members. I introduced the Jacksons to two Elders, Brother Long and Brother Fleming. Fleming, who had deep pockmarks all over his face and flirty blue eyes, was younger than the other Elders and grotesque in a handsome kind of way. Natalie had told me he had a colostomy bag. I found this fact about him intriguing—the bag was undetectable, no matter how hard I tried to find signs of its presence.

While Katherine was engaged in conversation with the Elders, I showed La Toya and Michael the bookstore and introduced them to a few of the youth. Of course, the Rolands were as annoying as ever with their gushing.

"It's so good to meet you!" Natalie enthused. "We've heard so much about you."

I was dying to whisper to Michael that they were huge fans of the Osmonds, knowing that they were a thorn in Michael's side, but I held back.

I could see the strain on La Toya and Michael's faces as they inched toward the exit.

Michael looked at me and pantomimed holding a telephone up to his ear with one hand and pointing at me with the other.

Suddenly, I was approached by Brother Long and Brother Fleming, who asked to speak to me in their private chambers.

The two Elders sat me in a small, nondescript office, the same one where the baptism questions were posed.

"Sister Darls, can you tell us a little about how you conduct your studies with Michael?" Brother Long asked.

I explained that we used the Bible study aid, *The Truth that Leads to Eternal Life*, just as I did with Tina, and that we took turns reading the paragraphs and then discussed the important points. I didn't volunteer that we did more talking and joking than actual Bible studying.

"We know you're newly baptized and a dedicated servant of Jehovah," Brother Long said. "You have the knowledge required, but it's important to understand certain issues might arise due to the high-profile nature of the Jacksons. We'll occasionally provide you with guidance and oversight."

I felt special that they were acknowledging my qualifications and abilities. At the same time, I was anxious to leave the office. Typically, being called into that office alone with the Elders meant a reprimand, and I didn't want anyone to get the wrong impression—especially after what had happened to Ken Lewis.

After coming out of the Elders' private chambers, I went outside and found Michael under a tree. With one hand gripping the trunk, he swung, circling close to me and then farther away, each time moving in a bit more. He came up to my face and then swung back. He was so close; I could feel his breath on my mouth. My knees weakened. *Is he going to kiss me right here in the parking lot of the Kingdom Hall?*

We were so close I could barely breathe, and at that moment Katherine and La Toya approached and Michael, grinning widely, did a graceful leap toward the car.

I lingered in that moment for days, the memory of his face so close to mine. *What if he does like me? Or was that him just teasing and being hyped up from the meeting?*

Michael called me that night.

"Hi, D. I really enjoyed the talk today, and so did Mother and La Toya. Mother called Rebbie in Kentucky and let her know we'd be going to meetings more regularly. What did you do after the meeting?"

"Well, Jesus ordered this in Matthew 28:19: 'go make disciples of all the nations, warning people that Armageddon will happen soon.' So, I went out into service after the meeting, going door to door to teach people about our beliefs."

"How does it work?" he asked. "Do you just pick an area?"

I explained that we all had assigned territories and map printouts, and the system was organized to ensure we covered all the neighborhoods of LA repeatedly. "It feels so important with how little time is left," I said. "Armageddon is only a few months away!"

"Do you think we can go out in service together?" he asked.

"What about being recognized? What if someone asks you for your autograph?"

"I'll wear a disguise." He giggled. "I have a pair of big dark glasses, a mustache, and a wig that I use sometimes on the road."

What a fun idea! "I think that could work," I said as evenly as possible, trying to keep my cool. "Do you wanna go out in service with me next week?"

"Yes!" he said, adamantly. Then, after a pause, "Hey, D, I was thinking today about faith and belief in Jehovah. If you compare faith in God with how a caterpillar transforms into a butterfly, it makes so much sense. We know what will happen even when we look at the cocoon. We never question it because we have faith. We believe it will change."

ONE MORE FOR THE FLOCK

On January 1, 1975, despite widespread belief that Armageddon would occur on New Year's Day, we were all disappointed: the day passed without incident. And now the exact date of the event remained unknown, leaving many Jehovah's Witnesses in anticipation.

I expected the new year to be different, but everything felt pretty much the same. Susie graduated from Cal Prep mid-year. After a brief move to Florida and a stint working at Disney World as Sneezy from *Snow White and the Seven Dwarfs*, she returned home and found a job in the Valley as an aerobics teacher.

I was hoping to acquire another Bible student to continue my positive momentum. Some of my peers had two or three, and some even had study groups. Being highly productive in my reported hours was my guarantee toward securing salvation.

I had my eye on a girl at school as a potential candidate.

Cindy was new to Cal Prep. She had pink-dyed hair and a reputation for being into witchcraft and drugs. According to the school gossip mill, she spent time at graveyards gathering vials of dirt to cast spells. She didn't have many friends. Cindy wore heavy black eyeliner, and her pasty skin made her pink hair look even more dried-out, almost as if it were singed on the ends. She seemed like someone who could use some light in her life.

Since I worked in the office, I knew we lived on the same street. But Cindy lived on the south side of Ventura Boulevard, the side of green hills, long driveways, and hidden estates, while I lived on the north side—the side of carports, freeways, and two-story apartment buildings.

We were in line together for nutrition one day when Cindy looked at me and said, "I see you at the bus stop near my house. I could give you a ride sometimes if you want."

I was surprised, considering how much of a loner she seemed to be. But she also had a brand-new Ford Pinto, and getting a break from the bus was too tempting to say no to.

"That would be great!" I said with a tentative smile.

Once we began riding together, I learned that Cindy was an only child and her father was a wealthy businessman, much older than her beautiful mother. She mentioned there was a lot of drinking in her house, but she had her own wing in their huge ranch-style home.

"I come and go whenever I like," she said, shrugging. "They don't really keep track."

During our drives, I began to witness to her using the questions I'd learned to generate interest. When she complained about having few friends, I asked, "Would you like to know more about what the Bible teaches? Did you know we're living in the last days? Soon God will destroy the wicked and this earth will become a paradise in which people can live forever in perfect health among neighbors who really love one another." I was on a roll now, reciting my script. "Are you interested in hearing about the good news of a future filled with everlasting peace?"

"I'm an atheist," Cindy said.

I nodded. "Most religions are filled with hypocrisy—it's easy to get discouraged."

"What's different about your religion?" she asked. She seemed genuinely curious.

"We study the actual Bible, word for word, and have modern scholars helping us make sense of the scripture. The Bible is filled with predictions that are coming true right at this very moment. We don't believe in heaven or hell, just a paradise on earth without death, disease, or violence. Isn't that appealing?" *Who could say no to that? I thought.* "The Book of Matthew, Chapter 24 Verse 7, predicts the signs of the end of times during these critical days of famine, earthquakes, disease, crime, and war on a large scale. If you like, we can have a Bible study one day after school."

Over the next few weeks, Cindy grew more open to the idea—and within a short period of time, she became my second Bible student.

"You're doing so well in The Truth, Darls, and are a shining example for other young folks. Phil and I are so proud of you."

Susie and I were in the van with Tina and Phil, and I had just told them about my new Bible student. Susie was especially quiet during the ride. I was floating on a spiritual high, but Susie seemed less enthusiastic about The Truth lately and more interested in dance practice. I thought maybe my success in having two Bible students and getting so much praise was difficult for her.

Susie had been a little lost ever since graduating high school. She wanted to go to college in Santa Cruz and study dance, but the religion frowned on higher education, citing it as an unnecessary pursuit unaligned with the goals of a Jehovah's Witness. They didn't believe in ambitious endeavors, since there were so few days left before the End of Time. But because she was only seventeen, the Elders had to abide by the decision of my parents, who wanted her to go. So now she was applying for college next year. I only had one year until I graduated, but I hoped Armageddon would happen by then, so I wasn't thinking too much about the future beyond that.

I was scheduled this evening to give a presentation with Rosalie—a skit about Bible study. I had just gotten this assignment earlier in the day, filling in last-minute for another member.

When we got to the Kingdom Hall, we sat with Rosalie. I looked around to see where Michael was sitting. I spotted him in the row to my left and we locked eyes. He nodded toward the stage with his chin and gave me a big smile. He and I had worked on the talk together during our study that afternoon. I had another talk scheduled with Susie for next week. My life was becoming filled with works of faith.

Susie was moving around in her seat. She attempted to distract me by turning my pages in the songbook, making me lose my place.

I elbowed her and whispered, "Stop it"—but when I looked at her, I cracked up.

I said a silent prayer before going up on the stage with Rosalie. My biggest concern was walking up the steps with my back to the audience. My self-consciousness kicked in as tall, slender Rosalie walked in front of me. I imagined Michael's eyes on me. *He sees me all the time*, I told myself. *This isn't any different.*

As soon as I was seated, my focus returned, and Jehovah took center stage in my mind.

After the meeting, Elder Fleming approached me.

"Sister Darls, you are doing so well in The Truth. I can see you as a future Pioneer. I heard you were given this talk last-minute... well done." He put his hands on both my shoulders. "You looked so cute up there when you almost laughed and I saw you regain your composure. What was going on that made you almost laugh?"

Michael came up right then and shook my hand. "Excellent talk, Sister Darls."

His presence saved me from having to answer the Elder's question. What a relief; I didn't want to tell him that Michael almost cracked me up by crossing his eyes at me during the talk.

ARMAGEDDON

Michael and I spent a week of lunchtime Bible studies trying to get through a dense *Watchtower* article about the Tetragrammaton, the Hebrew consonants YHWH, and the origins of the name Jehovah. It was dull.

Michael defaulted to the familiar topic of the divide in our families. Armageddon was real to us and coming that year, even if we didn't know exactly when, and the fear of losing our families continued to plague both of us. It was comforting to know I wasn't alone. I quoted a familiar scripture from the Book of Peter, which predicted that some would be slow to accept God's message. The ability to access Bible verse and quote from memory was a pact I had made with Jehovah: I had promised to demonstrate my obedience to witness by spreading his word.

Michael repeated, "Peter, Chapter Three, Verse 9," and wrote it in the margins of his notebook. "Do you think your mother will ever step foot in a Kingdom Hall?" he asked. "Because honestly, D, I can't picture Josep doing that."

"There's no way on Earth I can picture my mother doing it, either," I said.

If he only knew how much my mother was disgusted by the religion or that she had a violent temper, forcing me to always walk on eggshells. We both held some stuff close to the chest, but I sensed his relationship with his father was similar. I saw the tension in his face and noticed his body stiffen when he spoke about Joseph. I recognized the pain, the sense of unworthiness, and the unspoken reality of the hurt nobody talks about. Michael started making circles and squiggly designs with a stick in a little puddle of water filled with leaves. Then he grabbed a few supple eucalyptus leaves, closed his eyes, and inhaled. I watched his long, dark eyelashes flutter.

After a meditative silence, he looked up and caught me staring. We locked eyes and grinned. I longed to say something impressive, something he'd enjoy, to break the tension.

"Have you ever seen how long the lashes are on a llama?" I said, knowing he had a fondness for llamas.

"Oh, D, I really want a pet llama," he said, his eyes shining. "They're special creatures. Did you know that? Their fur provides the softest and warmest type of wool. Many people in South America use it to weave blankets for protection from the elements and these people are gentle vegetarians. They don't need to harm the llama in any way to get the fur. God created such a perfect system for man to exist."

His enthusiasm for animals lit him up. He got so excited, he stood and started pacing.

"And, D, did you know their teeth grow so long they need to have them cut or they'd grow all the way to the ground? And one more thing—they spit when they're frightened."

He sat and sketched two llamas facing each other with spit flying between them. He turned the sketch around for me to see and we laughed.

"Your laugh has this thing, D ... there's a little throaty sound you make, like your laugh has a tail," he teased, and tried to imitate the sound.

We had spent that day's Bible studies discussing the gruesome murders of our family members at the hands of Jehovah and an impending violent war that would end our current civilization, and yet now, minutes later, we were screaming with laughter.

"Have you ever known anyone who's died?" Michael asked, suddenly sober again.

"Just one," I said. "My uncle."

I'd received a call from my oldest sister while I was working in the office at Cal Prep only a few days before. Uncle Kenny had died from a heart attack. He was the one who'd molested me a few years earlier. I felt no sadness at the news; I hadn't felt much of any emotion, to be honest. It had been a disappointing first-death experience; I'd always imagined I'd have a dramatic crying scene upon a family member's death.

"I can't imagine not seeing my family for eternity," I told Michael.

"Me either," he agreed. "My brothers and sisters are everything to me."

"Are they as important as a school is to a fish?" I asked playfully.

"They're as significant as a flock is to a seagull," he replied.

"Then they must carry the same weight as a pride to a lion."

Michael giggled, then looked up at a large bird that had swooped low, hovering close to our hiding place. With his gaze not leaving the sky, he talked for a moment about the marvel of a bird's aviation skills.

Michael never missed a chance to open my eyes to the subtleties of the natural world. It was like having my own personal National Geographic narrator. The world was so much bigger when we were together.

IN SERVICE

Michael came along in the van with Tina and Phil after the Sunday meeting to go out in service, better known as going door to door.

This was a crucial component of our religion's doctrine about the fast-approaching End of the World, which we called The Great Tribulation. We were obliged to give everyone on earth the opportunity to hear the message and thus have an opportunity to be saved. According to The Watchtower Society's interpretation of the scripture, Armageddon would not occur until everyone had a chance to hear the message of salvation. This was confusing to me because there must be so many unreachable people on earth—but when I brought this up to my mentors, they assured me that I should put all my trust in Jehovah.

It was a bright and sunny day with cottony, cumulus cloud formations hanging in the blue sky. Hitting the neighborhoods right after a meeting at the Kingdom Hall, we were pumped up with "God Juice." I was happy to be alive and part of the chosen few, and I sensed the same exuberance from Michael.

We traveled in car caravans to different neighborhoods, each one divided into territories. Witnesses covered their respective regions in groups. We had a rehearsed pitch—and on this day I was well prepared, knowing I'd be observed by my Bible student.

I was doing this without my parents' knowledge. They never would have allowed me to take such a risk with my safety, going into strange homes. I told myself it was okay because I was vigilant about staying in a big group and in constant communication with my fellow doorknockers. I encouraged Michael to always stay connected to the group and cautioned him against ever going into a house unless someone from the group knew. I felt protective of my new Bible student—and of course, famous as he was, he was precious cargo. It was a huge responsibility.

Michael brought a black-brimmed fedora and large sunglasses. They were kind of silly-looking and seemed like they'd attract more attention than they would deflect, but they made Michael feel safe.

We went to the first door, just the two of us. I knocked, and when a woman answered the door, I made the introductions.

"Hello, this is Brother Michael and I'm Sister Darls. Do you have a few minutes to hear a positive message?"

I really wanted Michael to see I was good at this and to demonstrate the skills needed to be effective.

"Are you concerned about the conditions of the world?" I asked the woman at the door without waiting for her to answer my first question. "Would you like to see an end to war and famine?"

The idea was to get the householder to say yes to several questions to condition them to say "yes" when we went in for the closing question: "Would you like to schedule a time for us to return so you can learn more about the New System promised by God?"

We didn't get that far at this house. The woman shut the door almost immediately, saying, "None of you Jehovahs, no thanks!"

As we walked away, I explained to Michael that this was a common response.

"I think you did a great job, D," he said. "You sounded knowledgeable but not too pushy." Then he admitted he had been nervous that she would want to talk more.

We cracked up at the irony of hoping for a "no" when the intention was to get a "yes."

At the next house, a man answered.

"Are you concerned about the condition of the world?" I asked him. "What with all the wars, hunger, poverty, and natural disasters, we could use some good news. Would you like to enjoy everlasting peace on earth?"

It's difficult to say no to that question. We were well-trained salesmen, taught to close a deal.

I held up a *Watchtower* magazine. The bright red cover showed hopeful faces of people, young and old, and the title "Better Times Ahead."

The man opened the screen door, reached for the magazine, and looked closely at it.

"If you'd like to learn more good news," I said brightly, "I can have Brother Phil return next week to discuss what you've read and answer any questions."

I was confident now, and I was enjoying showing Michael how to successfully place Bible literature.

At one house, Michael was recognized; I was surprised it didn't happen more often. When asked if he was Michael Jackson, he simply replied, "Yes." It seemed like it was no big deal, and it did help get the magazine accepted at that house.

By the time we were finished that day, we'd placed four magazines and one Bible study aid book. I was brimming over with faith, and sharing this with Michael solidified my convictions to pursue The Truth even harder.

That night, Michael called to thank me for taking him along in service. Thankfully, I was the one to answer the phone; I didn't want my mother to pick up and say anything that might embarrass him. My father looked at me with a grin and helped unravel the phone cord as I dragged it to my bedroom for privacy.

"D, this was an incredible day, and I want to be even more involved when I'm not traveling," he gushed. "Thank you for taking the time to teach me. You're so good at going door to door. Do you think I'll ever advance to the place where I have my own Bible students?"

I loved being the one to show him the ins and outs of being in service. I felt masterful and had a sense of pride given to me by my faith.

If we both stay the course, I thought, *it's conceivable that one day we could be a team—a strong Witness couple, a force for Jehovah—just like Tina and Phil.*

If we remain steadfast in the Truth and survive Armageddon . . . we might even get married one day.

KINGDOM HALL

Not only was Michael going door to door, but Marlon came to a meeting the following week— La Toya told me he'd become more curious about The Truth.

After the meeting, I was on my way to greet Marlon when Brother Long approached me. I could see by the serious look on his face that I wasn't going to be getting the typical praise for being a stellar teen Jehovah's Witness.

It was a chilly evening, yet Brother Long was wiping sweat from his brow with a yellowed hanky. I noticed, looking up at him, that he had a little bush of hair growing out of each ear.

"Sister Darls, may I have a private word with you?" he asked in a somber voice, then led me to the corner of the hall.

"There's a general concern and dissatisfaction," he said, "with the length of Michael's hair."

Brother Long was the mouthpiece for all the Elders. He was calling me to a private meeting to voice a unanimous complaint that Michael's hair was too long for him to go out in service. The dress code for Jehovah's Witnesses was very conservative. Michael stood out with his trendy, large afro hairstyle.

Singling me out to relay the message showed that my influence on Michael had been fully noted by the governing body of our Kingdom Hall in Sherman Oaks—and perhaps even all the way to The Watchtower Society in New York. In this moment I got my first nervous inkling that I, along with Michael, was being closely observed.

I had difficulty responding. "Um, okay, Brother Long," I said finally, "I guess I can have a talk with him." But I had no idea how to approach this, and I wondered why they chose me—a fifteen-year-old girl—to deliver their admonition. I was horrified by the prospect of saying something critical to Michael. He was my best friend—and anyway, my reprimand would look insignificant stacked up against the advice of his team of show business advisors.

But I couldn't say no to the Elders. One way or another, I was going to have to do what they asked.

After a full day of tormenting myself on how to handle this, I went to Tina. I told her I was afraid of discouraging Michael; she reminded me to have faith and trust the Elders because they were mouthpieces for Jehovah.

I trusted Tina, but this felt like an overwhelming responsibility.

The following day, I mustered up the courage to call La Toya and tell her what Brother Long had said to me. She asked me to hold on while she went to get her mother, Katherine. They both got on the line. I was relieved that she was there to help with this issue. It felt bigger than I could handle.

"It's not your fault," Katherine said, but I could feel her mama bear instincts kicking in; she wanted to protect Michael and his sensitive nature. She was contemplative and quiet as La Toya asked me questions.

"What do they expect you to do, Darls?" she demanded. "He has a show business career. I don't understand why they didn't come to Mother directly!"

They were both upset with how the Elders were using me as the messenger. I didn't mind that; I was just relieved that they were not upset with me. We were all concerned that telling Michael this could cause him to be *stumbled*, which is the term used when someone leaves the religion.

We ended our call without having come to any real resolution about what to do.

La Toya called me later that night and was still very angry; like Katherine, she was defensive of Michael. She said they had decided to sit on the matter for now, because Michael had a big trip coming up.

After Michael came back from his trip, though, the issue disappeared, despite the fact his hair remained the same.

It's possible the Elders' backing off was motivated by money. Witnesses were encouraged to tithe 10 percent of their income to the religion, and I often noticed Katherine discreetly depositing an envelope in the donation receptacle at the back of the Kingdom Hall. Losing Katherine Jackson's contribution would have had a significant negative impact on the Church. They must have realized their mistake and that's why it was never brought up again.

Still, it was so stressful. I tried again to get support from Tina and Phil, but their answer was always the same: I must rely on the Elders without question. This left me confused. I started feeling doubt, but I was unsure about *what*, exactly. I didn't agree with how the issue with Michael had been handled. Why had they used me as the messenger instead of one of the Elders, who held authority and should've taken the lead? I felt used.

Applying logic to this situation conflicted with the Church's constant admonishment to rely on faith, and I was bothered by my inner struggle. As a Jehovah's Witness I was confident I was in The Truth, and that there could be nothing as solid and foolproof. I didn't want to experience even a small crack in my faith—so I took this as a cue to work even harder.

AT HOME WITH THE JACKSONS

A few days later, I went home with the Jacksons after school.

We rode in their customized blue-and-white van, driven by their chauffeur, Bill Bray. I climbed into the van in the school parking lot and as I disappeared into the back, I looked out the window to see who might be watching me. I was hoping to incur some envious reactions from the student body. As someone used to riding the public bus, I felt at that moment like somebody important—an insider and exclusive guest on this magic carpet of a ride.

Bill was a kindly older gentleman who transported the Jackson kids to and from school daily and pretty much everywhere they went. He had worked with the family for years, and I sensed the familiarity in his easy, playful interactions with them. As we drove to their house, the eight-track blasted "You Make Me Feel Brand New" by the Stylistics and the Jackson kids sang along in their highest-pitched voices, matching the falsetto chorus.

Michael poked me in the ribs a few times, until I eventually joined in.

Singing along with the Jacksons wasn't something I had ever imagined happening in my lifetime. I'm not a good singer—can't carry a tune—but we'd already participated in sing-alongs at the Kingdom Hall together. As Michael, Randy, and Marlon sang strong and loud, I practically mouthed the words, allowing very little sound to escape.

We approached their Encino home; Bill pressed a remote and the tall white gates opened. Security cameras faced a group of half a dozen or so teenagers who were crowded around the entry. The Jacksons smiled and waved at their fans and we headed down the long, palm tree–lined driveway. I was struck by how appreciative they were of the attention, contrary to what I had imagined—that it would be a nuisance to them.

"There's the girl from Michigan," Michael said. "I talked to her on Saturday. She has a brother that was born without a leg; she showed me his picture."

Once more, I was moved by his compassion. I wondered how this young man, my peer, had become so conscious of the suffering of others.

It seemed as if we drove a mile before reaching their house. Through the trees, there was an expanse of lawn that looked like a small soccer field and an asphalt area with a basketball hoop. The landscaping was manicured and perfect. The soaring cypress trees provided privacy from the neighbors.

I was less impressed by the high security and expansive grounds than by the simple fact that my best friends had finally invited me to their house. The tenets of the religion admonished us to interact only as necessary with non-Witnesses. Other than me, Michael and La Toya didn't have Witness friends, and I got the sense Katherine enjoyed my connection with her kids and had possibly encouraged the invitation. Recently, at the Kingdom Hall, she had asked me when I was coming to the house for a visit.

As we neared the house, Michael and La Toya looked toward the end of the driveway where the cars were parked and announced in unison, "Josep's not home!"

Michael winked at La Toya.

"Mother's here," he said, looking out the window at a red Mercedes sedan.

Bill parked the van in the large circular driveway, and we disembarked, one at a time. I was last and Bill held out his hand to balance me as I stepped down from the van. I wondered if he felt my hand shaking.

The house was a large, one-story, Tudor-style building with patterned stonework and several sliding glass doors. It wasn't the mansion I'd expected to find behind the iron gates.

To begin my tour, Michael and La Toya showed me around the outside first. Behind the house was a huge swimming pool with a diving board, and on the lawn was a badminton net with a couple rackets and shuttlecocks strewn in the grass. Farther down the driveway was a cottage that served as a music studio, equipped with all the latest recording equipment and a wall of gold records, music awards, and tons of photos of the Jacksons posing with other musicians and celebrities.

I noticed how young Michael was in so many of the photos and saw a sadness behind his smile—an incongruent expression I was coming to recognize and understand. I occasionally saw that same smile when he described how busy he was going to be working on a weekend or after school.

The front of the house boasted a grand entrance, with stone steps and carved, oversize double doors. But it seemed everyone used the sliding glass doors on the side of the house, which led directly to a sunken family room with cushy brown leather couches, a gigantic TV, and floor-to-ceiling speakers.

Behind the couches, on the upper level of the room, the dark ceramic-tiled floors were shiny, clean, and furnished only with a pair of his-and-her peacock rattan chairs reminiscent of Morticia's from the Addams Family.

The Jacksons' family room was the entertainment center, the nucleus of the home, a warm and welcoming place that hosted gatherings of family and friends—and the place where I'd come to spend a great deal of time in the next few years.

Michael and La Toya ushered me past the bar area, an enclosure separated from the family room by another sliding glass door. This is where Michael's cockatoo, Ricki, resided, in and out of his cage. Michael had taught him to talk and sing.

As I passed him, the brightly colored bird squawked, "Hi there, cutie, can I have a kiss?"

The unexpected greeting startled me, and I jumped.

Michael laughed, pointing at me. "I wish I had a picture of your face right now!"

The other side of the family room opened to the massive kitchen, with a cozy red leather booth where Katherine was sitting. She stood up and welcomed me with a long hug. "I hope you're staying for dinner."

Michael and La Toya hadn't said anything about dinner. I giggled. *Argh!* I was trying to break the habit of my nervous laugh when I didn't know what to say.

"Let's go hang out in my room for a bit," Michael said. "Walk this way." He performed the old Marx Brothers' joke of walking like Frankenstein in front of me. He turned around to see if I joined him; I hadn't. He seemed disappointed by my lack of playfulness, but I was too tense to play along.

On the way to his room, we passed through the living room, which seemed less used and somewhat formal, filled with seemingly brand new white crushed velvet couches, a few sculptured busts of famous Black people including Martin Luther King, and nondescript landscape oil paintings.

In Michael's room, encyclopedias and a variety of hardcover and paperback books, textbooks, and magazines spilled from numerous bookshelves. Other than the bookshelves, the room was tidy. His bed was neatly made; I wondered if he made it himself. Like a typical teenage boy's room, posters were plastered all over the walls, but the posters weren't of athletes, cars, or rock bands; they were all exotic birds, tigers, and cheetahs.

Michael was a big fan of anything Disney and had a slew of memorabilia. He picked up a Mickey Mouse statue. "Did you know that Walt Disney originally named him 'Mortimer'?"

"I had no idea." I was surprised by just how much Disney stuff he had. There were no framed celebrity photographs or any other signs of his life as a performer in his bedroom. *He wants to be so much like everybody else, when the rest of us want to be special like him,* I thought.

My nerves were beginning to calm. Michael must've sensed the shift because he moved toward me, so close that I could feel the heat of his body.

I broke the tension by reaching for a Minnie Mouse statue. "Did she used to be named something other than 'Minnie'?"

Michael threw his head back and laughed. "Good question, but I don't think so . . ."

He sat down on the bed, pushing aside a row of Disney stuffed animals to make room for himself. I normally would've thought it was weird for a sixteen-year-old to have a stuffed animal collection, but there was nothing typical about Michael. He was attached to things that belonged to childhood in a way that seemed full of longing for the years show business had stolen from his formative days. He pulled a Shel Silverstein book down from the shelf called *Lafcadio: The Lion Who Shot Back.*

"I want to show you some of the illustrations," he said.

I stood for a few awkward moments, wondering if I should sit down, until Michael patted the bed next to him.

The mattress sank a bit when I sat, and we bumped shoulders. I got a faint whiff of his cologne; it smelled soapy and clean.

Michael turned the pages of *Lafcadio* and explained how these kinds of drawings were done. "They're simple pencil sketches, but see how he conveys such great expression with just a few lines?"

He knew so much about art and was fascinated by its power to move people and elicit emotional responses.

La Toya came to the door. "Darls, come on, I want to bring you to my room."

"We're not finished yet; you need to wait your turn, cuz you're being a piggy," Michael teased her.

La Toya laughed. "Stop teasing, Mike, or I'll tell Darls my nickname for you."

"Don't you dare, Toya, or I'll have to torture you slowly," he said softly, laughing back. He put the book back up on the shelf, then turned back to his sister. "Bring her into the dining room when you're done," he instructed with a mischievous smile. "I have something to show you, D."

"Oh, yeah," La Toya said, "we brought back some goodies from Jamaica!"

"Toya, you ruined the surprise!" Michael mock-scolded her. "Now for sure I'll have to administer torture, including you singing *a cappella* a song of my choice while standing in the driveway until I say stop."

They continued to tease each other for a few minutes as I looked around, taking in more details of Michael's bedroom. It was an inside view of him, and I wanted to drink in as much as I could.

At Home with the Jacksons

La Toya and Janet shared a room with twin beds. It was sparsely furnished and had a deep, white shag carpet and gold-framed mirrored closets. There was not one bit of clutter, and I couldn't imagine where they put all their stuff—especially La Toya, who seemed to never wear the same outfit twice.

The only kids still living at home were La Toya, Marlon, Michael, Randy, and Janet. The older brothers were all married and had their own homes, mostly nearby.

After giving me a bedroom tour La Toya walked me into the dining room, where Michael was seated at the table, which was completely covered with black-and-white portraits. They had just returned from a concert tour in Jamaica, and Michael had taken hundreds of photographs of children while they were there.

"D, most of these children don't even own shoes." His voice was soft. "They live in mud shacks and rummage through the garbage for food."

He explained that the country's recent political unrest and independence had created more poverty and homelessness than ever, with children being the most affected. He focused on an image of a little boy beaming with pride as he held his baby sister. The boy was barefoot and had on a ragged, ripped skirt hiked up under his arms.

"He's ten years old," Michael said, pointing to his photo. "His name is Jahvonee."

"That's a pretty name," I said. "I wonder if it's somehow related to Jehovah."

Michael nodded. "I wondered the same thing."

As I continued poring over the photos, Michael provided a narrative for many of the kids. He knew their names and ages, and details about their living situation. His eyes brimmed with tears as he spoke.

After he was done telling me the children's stories, we walked the length of the table and circled a few times, viewing each picture in meditative silence. I was drawn to his compassion and interest in things other boys his age simply overlooked. Later, La Toya told me that Michael had spent every free moment he had while they were in Jamaica with the children in those photos, playing a street game with them and giving them money and candy.

On one of the chairs were a few wrapped gifts they'd brought me back. I unwrapped a straw purse shaped like a fish and discovered a few Jamaican coins inside.

"For good luck," Michael said.

LLAMA LINDA

During nutrition break the next day, Michael, La Toya, and I talked about their family dynamics.

The conversation began with a discussion about which family members were performing onstage in Las Vegas for their upcoming show. The Jackson 5 had just left Motown for CBS Records. The Vegas show was part of their public relations campaign to establish a new identity as a group. Randy, La Toya, Janet, and Rebbie had joined the group; the only missing sibling was Jermaine, who was married to Motown founder Berry Gordy's daughter.

Jermaine leaving the group had shaken Michael to his core and he had difficulty talking about it without choking up. But as was his way, he steered away from negative talk and gossip. "It will all work out, I just know it," he said repeatedly. He was disciplined about what he said in conversation—careful not to relay any criticism, consistently seeing silver linings.

"Jermaine hasn't been by the house since we started rehearsals for Vegas," La Toya said. "Mother is so hurt."

"Jermaine has wanted to go solo for a while now," Michael added. "I know he's going to be so successful. We need to believe in him, Toya."

While it was interesting for me to hear about the inner workings of their family, I was also thinking about how much I wanted to go to Vegas to see them.

As if picking up on my thoughts, Michael said, "I hope you and Sue can come to the show, Darls. It would be so fun."

I will make it happen, I thought. *No matter what.*

We had a half-day at school, so Michael and I went to our secret spot for a lengthy Bible study.

"D, do you think there'll be every species of plant and animal life that ever existed in the New System?" he asked me. "I wonder if dinosaurs will return. Did you know that they're prehistoric birds?" His eyes flashed with enthusiasm. "And did you know condors are the largest bird on the planet with a wingspan of up to ten feet? They're an endangered species. I donated to a wild animal sanctuary, and they sent me a poster of a condor. It's in my room. They can live to a hundred and mate for life."

"No wonder they're almost extinct," I quipped.

He threw me a look. "No, it's because the feathers are very valuable, and poachers kill them for money."

"What would you name your llama, Michael?" I asked, changing the subject. "Hmmm, I don't know," he said. "What do you think?"

"How about... Linda?" I replied. "Llama Linda."

His face lit up. "That's it!"

Later that night, Michael called and suggested we write a song together. "We'll call it 'Llama Linda,'" he said.

I explained to him that I knew nothing about songwriting, but he persisted.

"It's easy," he said. "We'll write the lyrics together and I'll find the melody. It'll be a collaboration."

Michael often spoke of his love for the power of a good melody and he said it was a unique creative expression, a vehicle to take the listener to a higher place. For him, everything was about coming closer to God. He was reverential toward all creatures. He said his favorite songs had melodies with tones that matched the rhythms found in nature, because they made him feel as if he could hear music emanating from the physical world.

"Listen," he said, "the first part came to me on the way home from school." He began to softly hum. The beat was simple, and he counted it out for me. "Can you feel it, D?"

"I *can* feel it. That sounds so good!" And it did. I could also feel myself falling harder for him.

"Can you come over tomorrow after school before I leave town?" he asked. "We can go into the studio and start writing the words. If you have any ideas tonight, don't forget to write them down."

The next afternoon, I found myself in the Jacksons' music studio with Michael.

We sat at antique wood-and-metal school desks with attached chairs. Michael opened a notebook with a few torn pieces of lined paper where he'd scribbled some lyrics. He put a page in front of me, and immediately my eyes were drawn to the words he'd scratched out; I was curious to learn more about his creative process.

"Will you read the lyrics out loud?" I asked.

The song was about a young llama named Linda who disobeyed her mother. She and her three younger siblings were accompanying their mother on a trek for food, without the protection of their father. Llama Linda was told to pay attention and stick with the pack, but to please her mother, decided to go scavenging for a bounty of fruit for the family. She got distracted by low-hanging fruit and wandered away from the pack. The rain began to pour, turning into sheets of hail. The rest of the llama pack ran ahead for shelter, leaving Llama Linda behind. The lost llama sat under the fruit tree and cried, soothing herself by eating the fruit.

I wondered if this reflected Michael's relationship with his father. Then another idea occurred to me: What if Llama Linda was really *Michael*, the child who worked, and the fruit in the song was a metaphor for the fruits of his labor, bringing support to the family? Michael intermittently looked out the window with an almost obsessive frequency, checking to see if Joseph was coming home.

I wanted to share my theory, but the code of silence we followed about the sins of our parents prevented me from asking directly.

"The chorus goes like this," he continued. "*Llama Linda, she lost her way, scared of the thunder and the price she'll pay...*" He paused. "But it needs one more line that will rhyme. She's more scared of getting in trouble with her father, who's very strict, than of being wet and lost."

"How about this, Michael? *Scared of the thunder and the price she'll pay, when Father Llama hears about her day.*"

"D—that's perfect!" Michael grinned. "See? You really *are* a songwriter!"

The unexpected compliment boosted my confidence.

For the next hour we toyed with the lyrics, cracking each other up with silly ideas and nonsense. Michael sparkled. He was earnest, talented, intelligent, and kind—and to top it off, we had a *real* connection.

"Wait," he said suddenly, "I forgot the most important part, D: the melody."

He hummed and sang *la-la-la*, culminating in *la-la-Llama Linda*. He did this a few times, and each time he got to *Llama Linda* he drew out the line in a long, slow fade: *Lindaaaa*...

Every time, I was struck by the beauty of his sweet voice.

When Michael felt we were ready to record, he directed me to sit on the bench in front of the massive sound mixer console. He began tinkering with the controls. There seemed to be a thousand buttons, knobs, and faders. Michael switched back and forth between them every which way with complete expertise. This was a side of him I didn't know: Michael the sound engineer.

He tapped the microphone. "Testing, testing, Darls and Michael, testing, testing, Llama Linda."

Michael understood music like it was a chemistry formula; he had a deep love for melodies and harmonies, and was always experimenting with notes and putting together sounds as if there were an orchestra in his head. I loved sitting close to him on the bench and seeing the muscles in his leg flex under his trousers as he pressed on the floor pedals.

If we really have one soul mate in life, I thought, *Michael must be mine.*

I felt so deeply connected with him while at the same time filled with doubt. Michael put a microphone in front of me. "Now that you know the lyrics and the tune well enough, go on and sing the first part of the song, D." He smiled in anticipation, with both hands resting on the sound board faders.

I was reluctant—quite self-conscious about my singing—but I followed his instructions and slowly Michael made me feel at ease. He pushed a fader, and my voice echoed. With his magic touch, I sounded better than I'd ever imagined possible.

He added a rhythmic drumbeat, and we sang the lyrics in harmony. His voice carried mine. We swayed together, shoulder to shoulder, mastering our masterpiece. Lost in the moment and now fully present with me, Michael stopped glancing out the window. I wondered if this was what it was like to fall in love.

"This was so fun, D," he said as we finished yet another run-through. "I wonder what time it is. There's a movie I want to record."

La Toya came in just then, breathless. "Michael, Mother says come in now. I mean it, now! Right this minute!" Her voice was even higher than usual, and she seemed especially anxious. "Josep is coming home, and the musical you wanted to record is about to start!"

Michael moved with quick precision, shutting down the sound board and turning off the lights. His manner changed and he became serious while focusing on a quick exit.

We grabbed our stuff and hurried into the house.

"What does that mean, 'record'?" I asked as we entered through the sliding glass door.

Ricki, the cockatoo, squawked, "Record!" and we were both a little startled.

"C'mon, you'll see, it's so great," Michael said, rushing to put his stuff in his room.

Minutes later, Michael, La Toya, and I convened in the family room to watch a movie.

Before we sat down, Michael showed me an electronic device called a VCR. He was enthralled with the technology and demonstrated how it worked. He held a huge black cassette, slid it into the recorder, and pressed a button before turning on the old Fred Astaire/Ginger Rogers movie he wanted to watch. This was a *completely new* concept to me, the idea of being able to rewatch something at one's leisure. I was fascinated and wondered how much this kind of thing might cost.

When we'd finished watching the movie, Michael pressed a button on the bulky recorder and rewound the tape to a solo Fred Astaire dance sequence. Then he ran up the steps to the upper tiled part of the family room and faced the TV. As Fred Astaire danced on screen, Michael recreated the routine, step for step, in front of our eyes, in perfect sync.

My eyes moved back and forth from his feet to the TV in astonishment. Michael had memorized the full sequence after only one viewing. This was the first time I truly understood his dance genius.

Michael had recently mentioned wanting to pursue acting. He loved musicals and we shared an obsession with *The Wizard of Oz*. He put that recording on next, and as it played, he abruptly stopped it here and there, freezing frames to point out details—all the things La Toya and I might have missed.

"D, do you see the umbrella strapped to the bike of Aunt Em's mean neighbor?" he asked me, pointing at the screen. "Later she plays the Wicked Witch, and that's a foreshadowing of when she melts from her contact with water."

I'd seen this movie countless times and never noticed this.

"My favorite character is the Scarecrow," he said during a later pause, "because even though he wants to get a brain from the wizard, he's the wisest of them all. What character would you be in *The Wizard of Oz*, D?"

That was easy.

"Glinda the Good Witch, of course."

"Do you like Michael?" La Toya asked as she walked me out to the van.

I must've glanced over at Michael one too many times that evening. My face grew hot. "Only as a friend," I lied.

There was too much at stake to admit the truth. I risked my friendship with La Toya, who would surely be put off by my having a crush on her brother; and on top of that were the complexities of being Michael's Bible mentor and too young to date with the intention of getting married.

"Darls," La Toya said soberly, "Josep said you two are not to be alone together anymore."

I was shocked. "But why? Toya, what happened!?"

I saw Joseph come and go from the house, but he essentially ignored me. I could feel his hostility, and thought he was kind of scary, so I was relieved he didn't engage with me. Besides, he was rarely home when I was over.

"Mother said he's concerned that you and Michael could develop a romance," La Toya explained, "and he doesn't want Michael to marry a white girl."

"Marry?" I gaped at her.

"Yes. Someone told him that Jehovah's Witnesses get married as teenagers. He thinks you're leading Michael down the wedding aisle."

Joseph Jackson wasn't wrong about the intensity of my feelings for Michael, but that didn't include manipulation. I didn't realize how much our race difference meant for Joseph, so I had to ask myself, what did it mean for Michael? It hadn't ever seemed like a barrier for him. Still, my spirit was crushed by Joseph's edict.

"Mother said she thought this might come up, but since Joseph is hardly ever home lately, she was hoping he wouldn't notice."

"Notice what?" *What did I do wrong?*

"Darls, you and Michael spend so much time together—not only here but also on the phone and at school, which luckily Joseph doesn't know about. And when you're here, it seems like you like each other as more than friends."

I was glad she said "like *each other.*" At least I didn't look like a lovesick puppy in an unrequited relationship. *Maybe others noticing our closeness means that he really does like me.*

Even as I worried what Joseph's displeasure with our friendship might mean for me, I couldn't help but feel a little giddy over La Toya's words.

UNDER SURVEILLANCE

"I saw Brother Long talking to you today after the meeting," La Toya said.

We were standing in the Kingdom Hall parking lot after a Sunday meeting. Ever since the incident with Brother Long conferring with me about the length of Michael's hair, we'd been a bit on guard about private moments with Elders.

La Toya and Michael had been gone for a while, performing in Las Vegas. Susie and I had in fact managed to get a ride with friends to the show at the MGM Grand, and there was so much I wanted to catch up with them about. La Toya, Janet, and Rebbie were wonderful performers, and I had questions and observations for both La Toya and Michael. But that conversation would have to wait.

"Well, this time it's not about your brother, Toya," I told her. "Believe it or not, he wanted to talk to me about Susie. They told me she's being watched due to her—and I quote—'lack of Biblical seriousness and distracting conduct.'"

"What does that mean, Darls?"

"Well, while you were away, Susie and I were assigned a last-minute talk. Susie giggled uncontrollably the entire time."

Susie was blossoming into womanhood with a stunning beauty that earned her unusual amounts of attention from men and often negative attention from other women. She certainly had the good looks and height to make a realistic attempt at pursuing modeling, as our mother had repeatedly pointed out in recent years. But as much as Susie wanted an education or a career in modeling, the Jehovah's Witness ideology demanded a life of devotion to God and an abandonment of ambition. Susie seemed to be losing her grip on the religion as she looked toward her future.

La Toya's eyes grew big. "I wish I was there with you. You must've been so embarrassed. What're you going to do, Darls?"

Michael joined us then. "What's all the gossip about?" he asked.

"The Elders approached Darls 'cause they're worried about Susie stumbling from the faith," La Toya informed him.

This time it was Michael's eyes that widened with concern. "We have to leave now," he said, "but I'll call you tonight."

When Michael called that night, we talked about what might be going on with Susie. Michael said he was worried about her because she seemed uninterested in The Truth.

"I sat next to her at a meeting a few weeks ago and she kept trying to get me to play tic-tac-toe with her," he said.

He added that he hadn't wanted to hurt her feelings, so he took a *Watchtower* magazine and folded her tic-tac-toe paper into it and stuck it under his Bible. He said he understood her confusion, trying to figure out what to do when she graduated. I was impressed by his empathy and understanding of her unique situation. He compared her dilemma with his own, saying he didn't have a choice about his future after high school because he was part of a band. He had to continue what he was doing.

"Sometimes having too many choices can be a problem," he said. "I'm gonna offer to spend more time with her."

"What do you think of inviting her to join us for one of our Bible studies, Michael?"

I hoped he might have some influence over her but feared it might be too late.

"Perfect!" he agreed. "Let's do that."

But Susie was sick the following week and then the Jacksons left town again. Our plan never came to pass.

A few weeks later, the Roland family invited Susie and me, along with another Witness family, for a weekend on their cabin cruiser anchored at Catalina Island. After a long day of sunbathing and snorkeling, all the wives and girls went out shopping—except Susie, who had fallen asleep and was left behind. When we returned, we found Susie dancing provocatively in a red bikini to "Love to Love You, Baby" while the adult men in our group watched her like they were at a burlesque show. The back tie of her top was loose, exposing the sides of her breasts and threatening to come undone completely. There was an open bottle of vodka nearby and an empty plastic cup in Susie's hand.

I grabbed a beach towel, put it around her, and pulled her into the back room.

"Susie, how'd you get so drunk?"

"They gave me vodka and orange juice," she slurred. "They called it a screwdriver and said not to tell the ladies... oops, I just told."

I was worried for Susie and appalled that my friends' fathers were not behaving like Christians. They had taken advantage of a minor, and that scared me. I knew my own father, who was not even a Jehovah's Witness, would never disrespect a female in this disgusting manner.

I didn't know who to turn to for support, so I got Susie to put some clothes on, and together we laid down on the bed.

"Oh god, everything is spinning," Susie declared. She jumped up and ran to the bathroom to throw up.

Soon after, the adults went out to dinner while the kids stayed behind. At one point during the evening, Rosalie turned to me accusingly and said, "You know whose fault this is, don't you? Susie knows better than to wear a bikini."

Natalie nodded in agreement.

I was appalled by their hypocrisy. It was a turning point in my friendship with the Rolands.

After we got home, Mrs. Roland spread gossip blaming Susie for the entire incident, calling her a temptress. She left out the part about the men being drunk and giving her alcohol, of course.

GOING AWAY GIFT

I was beginning to feel the pressure of graduating and was sad that my lunchtime Bible studies with Michael would soon be coming to an end. La Toya and I were graduating and Michael had one more year. I was worried about losing my closeness with them in an unknown future. Although we saw each other outside of school, I was concerned that our connection would fade if we didn't have a reason to hang out every day.

I decided to give Michael a gift to represent the transition and my loyalty to him. I wanted him to know that our relationship had meaning and continuity. I selected a book by Shel Silverstein called *The Giving Tree* because it was about the growing pains and fears related to change and moving forward in one's life. I thought Michael would enjoy the illustrations since he loved the ones in Silverstein's book *Lafcadio* so much. The artwork also reminded me of Michael's own sketches.

I considered an inscription and after some back and forth jotted this down: *You've worked so hard to know The Truth. Thank you for being my friend and for letting me be a part of your spiritual quest toward Jehovah. I look forward to more studies! Darls.*

I wrapped the book in tissue paper, and at the beginning of our next Bible study, I handed him my gift.

He looked at it with surprise. "What's this, D?"

"It's a going-away present," I said.

"I'm always going away," he chuckled, "what do you mean?"

"No," I said, "I'm the one going away this time—from high school, anyway."

He unwrapped the thin green-and-white hardcover book with its shiny new book jacket. He smiled when he saw what it was and said, "Thank you, thank you, *thank you*."

These moments of friendship and a common love for Jehovah, I felt, were a bond stronger than any other. I believed in that moment that I would truly love Michael forever, because that was what was promised to us as Jehovah's Witnesses: eternity. Although this required an apocalyptic worldview, it was seductive in its promise.

Ironically, the current political climate felt end-of-the-world-ish. Nixon had resigned in disgrace the summer before; the country felt lost. It fed directly into a paranoia, a feeling of being unsafe. Our commitment to Jehovah and to each other provided us with a sense of security.

Michael read the inscription out loud. I didn't expect to be so moved, but tears came to my eyes.

We sat in our private eucalyptus hideaway and enjoyed the story of the boy and his "giving tree." Michael turned the book over and studied the photo of bald, ex-Marine Shel Silverstein on the book flap. I don't think either of us were aware that Silverstein was also a prolific songwriter who specialized in novelty and narrative classics like Johnny Cash's "A Boy Named Sue" and Dr. Hook and the Medicine Show's 1972 hit "Cover of the Rolling Stone."

Michael giggled at Shel's tough guy look. "It's kind of ironic that he writes books for children looking like that," he mused.

We spent that lunch reading *The Giving Tree* together. Michael flipped the pages as we sat, drinking in the illustrations.

"I like the way he did that, what he did with the line," he said, pointing at a particular element of a drawing with his long finger. He was always noticing things I would have never spotted.

When we finished the book, Michael closed it and looked at me. "What's most meaningful about it for you, D?"

"That we met under a tree behind Cal Prep," I said.

He smiled and paused for a moment. "For me, it's about the relationship between man and nature and how generous nature is versus how destructive man can be." He moved close to me and looked me straight in the eyes, so deep that I felt it in my toes. "Thank you from the bottom of my heart," he said gently. "We're not ending our studies. We can continue to have them over the phone. And we can also study at my house—you know, except when we need to be careful."

I could feel the light in him shining so brightly. I felt like an imposter—the teacher once again taught by the student. The gift deepened our commitment to continue to work toward saving the world, but he was really saving me. Michael's essence was having an influence on my life. He believed in me and made me believe more in myself.

As much as I continued to feel a strong, electric connection with Michael, I knew things were shifting. His father's condemnation of me had put me on full alert. I was trying so hard to manage my feelings for him, even as Michael was getting busier in his career. He had a big summer of travel in front of him. He was going to be home intermittently, and I prepared my heart for the separation. This was self-preservation on an unconscious level—me gearing myself up for a whole new chapter.

Even though I'd deeply miss Michael and La Toya, the truth was, I was aching to get out of high school. After graduation, still technically a minor and under my parents' guardianship, I was going to college—despite the Witnesses' view that under the New System, higher education would be unnecessary and professionals obsolete. The Elders had met with Tina and Phil regarding my situation but knew I had no choice but to obey my parents, who insisted I go to college.

I'd once thought that becoming a Pioneer and devoting 100 hours a month of service to Jehovah would be the best life choice for me, but now I was secretly relieved to be going to college. I'd been groomed by Ruth Yardum to attend a university for four years now, and I was graduating from Cal Prep as valedictorian. I planned to study special education and prepare for the orphanages that Michael and I spoke of—our shared vision for the future!

La Toya called the week before graduation and asked if she could come over and take me for a ride.

She arrived holding a copy of Michael's solo album, *Music and Me*. As I climbed into her car, she held it up. "Do you have any Jackson 5 albums, Darls?"

I didn't own any of the Jacksons' music, which I realized at that moment was kind of odd. I shook my head.

La Toya, unfazed, smiled. "I thought you'd enjoy this album. It's different from the Jackson 5 albums, because Michael is singing solo."

Her long pink nails covered his face, but I could see Michael was playing acoustic guitar and wearing a cool bracelet. Even though that photo had been taken shortly before we met, he looked so young.

La Toya explained that the album came out a few years ago but had never gotten off the ground because the record label hadn't promoted it.

"Let's go to Casa Vega," she said, abruptly changing the topic.

We slipped into a dimly lit leather booth. The dark interior of Casa Vega made it feel like a perfect spot to share secrets. This place was not meant for being seen; it was meant for clandestine meetings—a hiding place.

I had a huge secret to share, one that was extremely difficult to contain: Susie had a boyfriend, a worldly one.

La Toya ordered the "secret" flour chips, which weren't on the menu, with extra spicy salsa, also not on the menu. She used a small stack of paper cocktail napkins to absorb the excess grease on each chip, made a little pile of the "corrected" chips, and then delicately ate them, taking little bites.

We sat there for hours, watching several tables of diners come and go as we commiserated about our family dramas and what they might mean for our respective futures.

FIRST CAR FREEDOM

From the day I got my first car, I became a regular visitor to the Jackson home. In fact, it was the first place I drove—straight from the Cutter Ford dealership in Van Nuys. I used $800 from my first student loan check to pick out a faded yellow four-door Toyota Corona. It looked like a lunchbox and felt like it weighed 20 pounds.

On a new car owner's high, I picked up La Toya and Michael and we went for the first of many joyrides together. It was heaven—me behind the wheel with my two best friends along for the ride. While they were used to having fancy cars and a chauffeur-driven experience, my used Toyota represented a ticket to freedom for all of us. La Toya sat in front and Michael sat in the middle of the back seat.

"It's too bad we're leaving tomorrow, just when you get your own car," Michael said. The Jacksons were leaving for a rigorous summer tour across the US, including another two-week stint at the MGM in Las Vegas. He started humming *"We'rrrre OFF to see the Wizard . . ."* and lightly tapped a beat on the seat.

It really was a new chapter, being able to drive myself and escape into the world with autonomy. It was exhilarating. But at the same time, I was sad that my friends were leaving.

We drove down Ventura Boulevard a few miles and then back toward their house. I enjoyed every red light because it meant more time together. I'd just turned on my blinker to turn in to their driveway when Michael piped up again from the back seat.

"Why don't we drive to the top of the street before you bring us home?" he suggested.

I'd never been up there before. We cruised up Hayvenhurst Ave. into the hilly residential area above the Jacksons' home.

"If we go slow and look into one of these fields, we might see a deer," Michael said.

"Your little friend, Bambi," La Toya teased.

Eventually, we reached the end of the road.

"Let's park here for a minute," Michael directed.

I pulled over and turned off the engine.

La Toya turned to Michael. "Should we tell her now?"

He nodded.

"We have a huge secret," she said seriously.

Man, this is the Season of Secrets, I thought.

"Darls, you can't tell anyone, and I mean not a soul," La Toya said. "Only Michael and I know..."

"I won't, I swear," I promised.

"Marlon got married," she blurted out. "Josep will be red hot."

Married?! He was only eighteen!

We all sat there quietly. Big changes were happening, and we didn't know how to begin acknowledging them.

Michael broke the silence.

"Look, there's Bambi!" he said, pointing out the window.

La Toya and I both turned our heads in sync to look, but there was nothing there.

Michael laughed hard, enjoying his prank. La Toya and I joined in, until we were all howling so hard we were out of breath. These moments were made even more special considering the reality that life was changing all around us, and that we were all moving forward, expanding, and transitioning away from the safety of our little cocoon.

During the weeks the Jacksons were away, I fantasized about the university life I was heading toward.

I sat tethered to the record player, headphones drowning out the chaos of my family, listening to Michael's album in the living room. I wondered about my life as a college student, being around so many boys and away from my small, familiar world. Would I be tempted to flirt, to take risks? I was so curious about what it would be like to kiss a boy. The pull I felt toward Michael was only making me more frustrated. I had less of the "God feeling" that felt so pure, and I missed that strong connection with Jehovah.

Wanting to escape our hot, crowded upstairs apartment and waiting for the occasional breeze to cool off the room, I had found my retreat: *Music and Me*. I wondered why La Toya had given me this album filled with love songs. Was she trying to tell me something?

The songs were mostly intimate, slow, and packed with emotions, fitting with what Michael had told me about his love for ballads. They were his favorite types of songs to perform, he said, because the ballads told authentic stories about people and heartache. I listened to the song "With a Child's Heart" on repeat.

This is helping me formulate ideas about the future orphanages Michael and I will open, even though Armageddon is supposedly still coming this year, I told myself. *It could be any minute.*

I was lying to myself, because I was truly enjoying fantasizing over my crush.

I was proud of my new summer job at the Sherman Oaks Movie Theatre and especially enjoyed the perk of free movie passes. As soon as Michael and La Toya returned home, I invited them to join me one night. I was so excited to treat *them* for a change. We decided to see *Bambi*, of course, indulging Michael's love for Disney animation.

My biggest concern was the terrible haircut I had gotten since we'd last seen each other. Susie had clipped my hair into a short bob, and tragically, though accidentally, chopped my bangs so severely that I looked like a 1920s flapper.

Michael got in the car first, holding a bag. "I have something for you, D. It's a book about childcare." He looked at me strangely. "Is that a wig?"

I was mortified. "No, it was a mistake."

I could tell he was trying not to laugh. He pulled it off, which must have taken great self-control. Meanwhile, he handed me his present. It was a huge, hardcover manual called *The Encyclopedia of Childcare and Guidance*. On the inside cover there was a Jackson 5 sticker and a handwritten note: *This is a really good book, Darls. You could really use it in the future. Never buy modern books on children because the world gets crazier every day. They tell you how to discipline your children psychologically and that's not good.*

Under the message, Michael had signed his name in a big, messy scrawl. I was touched.

"Thank you so much..."

Just then, La Toya got in the car, took one look at me, and started laughing. "Okay, Darls, you can take the wig off now. Didn't you wear that in a school play last year?"

"It's not a wig, Toya—Susie gave her a haircut," Michael explained. "D, if I could cut my hair to match yours, I would," he said kindly. "But this mop won't lay flat like yours."

"You look so unique!" La Toya piped in.

I was aware of how much she protected her own hairstyle and how strongly it was connected to her identity. I had never seen her without a signature cloth hat sitting on the top of her long, curly locks. *Maybe I should try a hat until this disaster grows out*, I thought.

Michael, La Toya, and I filed into the lobby of the theater, excited to be reunited once again after their travels. I introduced them to my manager, who was impressed and flustered.

"We really love having Darls as our employee," he gushed. "She's so reliable and such a hard worker."

Michael giggled as we walked away. "He talked to us like we were your parents instead of your friends!"

I walked them into the theater to find our seats and then La Toya and I went back out to the concession stand to get two huge buckets of popcorn. Michael and La Toya *loved* buttered movie popcorn, as did I. Sometimes we'd run into a movie theater just to get a bucket of popcorn and not even see a film.

When we reentered the theater, Michael was sitting between two empty seats. I hoped he was making sure we would get to sit next to one another.

La Toya and I settled in, with Michael in the middle.

Throughout the movie, Michael's arm lightly touched mine on the armrest. Sometimes one of us moved, but each time that happened we slowly found our way back to mutual contact.

I felt my toes tingle when we touched. I didn't know how I could wait until marriage to explore any more of this physical attraction. It seemed impossible. I wondered what would happen if we weren't Jehovah's Witnesses. Most worldly teens at our school were already having sex.

I got up to go to the bathroom; when I came back, Michael was sniffling, and I saw tears coming down his face.

"I know why you left," he whispered. "You knew what was going to happen and you didn't want to see Bambi's mother get killed."

I nodded—but it was a lie.

I don't know what felt worse: lying to him or not being as broken up about the murder of Bambi's mother as he was. I had let Michael believe I was as sensitive as he.

The thought crossed my mind that I could potentially die at Armageddon, even though I was baptized. But at that moment, I was more concerned by what Michael would think of me if he knew the truth than I was with Jehovah's everlasting judgment.

SUMMER OF '75

We were almost halfway through 1975, the year of Armageddon, so there was tremendous excitement around the upcoming Divine Sovereignty Assembly taking place at Dodger Stadium.

This highly anticipated Bible conference would consist of hours of uplifting talks, costumed Biblical plays, and the introduction of new literature from the Watchtower Society, as well as stories of our fellow Christians overcoming persecution and hardship. The intermission and lunch breaks would offer time to socialize with different congregations from all over California while hundreds of baptisms took place in an above-ground pool.

The anticipation of the Assembly had been building up for weeks at our regular meetings. We were all hoping for new information about the End of Days.

When the weekend finally arrived, I went with Katherine, Michael, and La Toya. Susie had a modeling gig and couldn't go. She wasn't coming to meetings much anymore. I was excited to be going with the Jacksons but sad that Susie wouldn't be joining us.

We wore name tags with our first and last names and home congregation. Michael didn't put his last name on his tag. It simply read, "Michael J—Sherman Oaks Congregation."

It was a hot day, over 80 degrees by 9:00 a.m., and the stadium was packed. I hoped our seats would be in the shade. My nylons were tight, and I was wearing a long blouse made of heavy fabric. Polite, clean-cut volunteer brothers ushered the crowds in an orderly fashion.

As I took in the scene, I wondered if people would bother Michael. This was his first big Assembly, and I wanted him to have a positive experience.

Katherine and La Toya admonished him to stay between them as we walked to our seats in the stadium; they felt protective too, of course.

The Jacksons were pros at getting through a crowd, and they moved with skillful grace. Katherine had a barely noticeable limp from childhood polio, but she walked fast. All three of them wore large, dark sunglasses—but even so onlookers stared, their eyes migrating from Michael's face to his name tag.

I was embarrassed for them by the gawking. *No wonder Michael and La Toya are so shy*, I thought.

Once seated, I looked out over the crowd. Over 50,000 Jehovah's Witnesses were present, and the magnitude of the gathering took my breath away—a sea of people, all there to worship Jehovah.

To begin, we stood and sang, all in unison:

We are sisters, we are brothers, sons and daughters and more.
And I love you even though I never met you before.
Give me your hand. We're in the same fight.
You give me strength to carry on toward eternal life.

Michael and I exchanged glances, sharing our euphoria—that "god feeling" so often evoked by our studies and lengthy spiritual discussions on the telephone.

The opening talk began. It felt so intimate and familial, which indicated to me that we were most certainly in The Truth. The high filled me from head to toe.

"Human rule is obviously failing," the speaker said. "God's rule is not! His purpose is to rid the earth of all the unsatisfactory present-day governments and to replace them with His Heavenly Kingdom under Christ."

The main talk on the last day of the three-day Assembly delivered a message: "One World, One Government, Under God's Sovereignty—for mankind living in this troubled world of confusion and disunity!" The emphasis was on how poor and unsustainable global conditions were, so much so that the world would surely soon come to an end.

We believed it, along with the thousands of Jehovah's Witnesses around us. After three full days of Bible instruction, we were all exhausted—but also inspired to work even harder to be part of this massive spiritual revolution. We were all hoping for salvation, convinced we would be together forever in paradise once we survived the impending Armageddon.

And we needed to be prepared for it to happen at any minute.

During the talks, Michael sketched in his notepad. I think this was his way of shielding himself from being constantly observed. On the car ride home, he and I sat together in the back seat and he showed me his sketches: several of the crowd and the baptism pool, all containing thought bubbles conveying religious devotion.

I was gratified to see how Michael's faith was expanding. For my own part, I'd needed this Assembly for encouragement. I felt my faith needed a boost—not only because Susie was pulling away but also because I was going against Watchtower's counsel by attending college.

There was so much at stake.

That summer, the Jacksons and I began spending Friday nights at the Sherman Way Roller Rink with a bunch of other young Witnesses. Teen Witnesses were encouraged to gather in groups to keep them from "being led into temptation."

The skating rink was at the north end of the San Fernando Valley; I was the first to arrive that night and was already circling the rink when Michael skated up behind me.

Peter Frampton's song, "Baby I Love Your Way," was blasting and the lights were bright. Michael passed me and then pivoted to face me, gliding gracefully backwards; given that he was a professional dancer, it came as no surprise that he was better at skating than I was. But I wanted him to see I was a decent skater, too. I felt confident in my skills, having skated often when I was younger—I even owned my own pair of skates.

Just then, a girl approached quickly and collided with me hard enough that I fell right on my butt. Michael began to laugh but stopped himself when he realized I might be hurt and offered me his hand.

I could feel people staring as he helped me to my feet.

"Where's La Toya?" I asked, trying to play it off.

"She's finding the right shoes ... you okay, D?"

"I'm okay, no bruises," I said. *Except for my pride.*

I got off the rink and went to find La Toya, who was tying her shoes. "Kathy's coming tonight," she said. "I'm waiting for her."

I felt hurt that La Toya had invited her, and I didn't understand why she was trying to get closer with her. "See you out there," I mumbled, skating out alone.

Back in the rink, I said hi to a few Witnesses and then a slow Roberta Flack song, "Killing Me Softly," came on. The bright lights dimmed, and people quickly began to couple up. I was unsure what to do with myself.

At that moment, Michael skated up from behind me again, but this time he grabbed my hand. It felt so small in his large, secure grip. I hoped he didn't notice that my palm was sweating. As I skated alongside him, I couldn't help but focus on every little movement of his hand in mine. We skated side by side while Michael did a few fancy moves, like skating on one leg and bowing forward. I was beyond thrilled.

After the song ended, the lights came on and Michael swung me in a circle and let go of my hand. I went sailing forward, but I didn't need much of a push—I was already floating on air.

After the couples' skate, I went to the snack bar. While waiting in line, I saw the girl who'd caused me to fall earlier. She was conversing with a Witness girl I recognized from meetings. I was close enough to overhear their conversation; they were both planning to be the first to grab Michael's hand for the next couples' skate.

"Yeah, he'll be polite about it and then he'll go find that girl from his school" one of them said. "He always wants to skate with her. I don't get it. What does he see in her?"

I walked away, humiliated and hurt.

Of course, Michael couldn't really like me, I thought. *Those girls are right. I'm not good enough for him.*

Yet I was willing to continue to put myself through the torture of undeclared love. Michael meant too much to me at this point; I felt as though I had no choice but to stay close to him, even if only as his friend.

PART TWO
THE VOICE INSIDE

> If I give up the "Truth," I give up all the security and safeness. I give up my dearest friends La Toya and Michael, and I accept the fact that I will be a victim of juicy, malicious gossip.
>
> — Journal Entry October 11, 1976

> Michael called me tonight. It left me totally drained. I poured out my heart to him unreservedly, telling him everything. I don't know if he grasped it.
>
> — Journal Entry October 18, 1976

DINNER PARTY

Hello Dear Diary,

I have so much to do. Tonight, I am giving a dinner party for Michael and La Toya. I'm going to make chicken enchiladas. It's their favorite dish. I have the recipe, it seems hard. There are so many ingredients and so many steps! I'm going to make a shopping list and then go to the store to buy everything. I am also going to go and pick them up. La Toya called and asked if my mom is going to be here. She gets uncomfortable around her. I can understand why. I need to figure out a way to nicely tell my mother to make herself scarce. Susie said she would help me clean the house, but she is not very reliable. I am getting some records put aside because we talked about making a soul train line and dancing. I hope they don't mind being in our little apartment. I have butterflies in my stomach. La Toya has been here lots, but Michael hasn't been here before.

I agonized over every detail of the gathering—especially my mother's potential presence. I kept hinting and making suggestions, because I didn't know how to ask my mother to stay away for the evening.

Eventually, I complained to Susie, who went directly to my mom and told her that La Toya was afraid of her. This seemed to amuse her.

"You don't want me to meet your *boyfriend*, do you?" she needled me.

"He's not my boyfriend, Mom," I insisted. "He's my best friend and Bible study partner."

"You could've fooled me," she said, and finally agreed to give me and my friends some space.

I invited my little brother Mikey to the party; he was about the same age as Randy, and I thought they would be a good match.

That afternoon, I scanned our apartment with a critical eye. The furniture was oversized for the confines of the small apartment space. The sofa seemed outdated; the saggy, once-white cushions looked sad and dingy. After much consideration, I placed a throw pillow over a coffee stain and another over a cigarette burn, removed my mother's ashtrays, scrubbed the bathroom, and put away all the toiletries.

Only La Toya had seen the apartment before, and when she came over, she rarely commented on anything except the large portrait of my mother, hanging above the sofa.

"I just can't believe how pretty your mom was," she'd said more than once.

My mother wouldn't have appreciated the past tense. I wondered if Michael would think my mother was pretty, and what La Toya might have told Michael about where I lived.

Once the apartment was in order, I spent a long time considering which albums to play. I decided on the Ohio Players, Donna Summer, the O'Jays, and Gladys Knight and the Pips, whom we all loved—especially the album *Imagination*, which included the songs "The Best Thing That Ever Happened to Me" and "Midnight Train to Georgia." The Jacksons and Gladys Knight shared parallel experiences as Motown bands. I put my new favorite album—Michael's *Music and Me*—away and out of sight.

Around 5:00 p.m., I looked around and sighed with resignation. It would have to do.

I picked up my guests shortly before six and took them back to my place. We pulled up out front and darted up the building stairs, where Susie waited at the door to greet us.

The Jacksons didn't flinch at our modest apartment. Michael complimented the vibrancy of my mom's potted plants and appreciated the black-and-white framed photos of my mother in her Carmen Miranda headdress from her days as a showgirl in Cuba. "It must've been hard to dance without falling over in that thing!" he commented.

We sat down to dinner almost immediately, but before eating we paused for Michael to say a prayer.

He closed his eyes, and we did the same.

He said nothing.

We waited, awkwardly, for a few moments.

"Michael," La Toya broke in, "hurry up. The food will get cold."

"Participation in prayer is always more important than partaking in food," Michael said. He closed his eyes again. "Now we will give thanks to Jehovah."

Michael then recited a heartfelt prayer focusing on the importance of friendship, calling it a gift from God. He declared that this would be one of many meals we would share when we were all together in the New System.

"And Jehovah," he continued, "we ask you for ongoing support and guidance to keep us all on track, because worldly temptations are many."

I understood that was for Susie—just like we'd agreed on in advance. This was part of our strategy to get her back to the Kingdom Hall.

Michael offered a special thank you to me for sweating over a hot stove to prepare that evening's meal, then closed with, "In Jesus's name. Amen."

After dinner, we cleared the table and Susie put on the first record. We lined up in parallel and then one person moved down the middle, originating a dance move that everyone else had to imitate, one at a time, also moving down the middle.

Michael insisted I go first.

I prided myself on being a decent dancer, having grown up with family dance parties and choreographing shows with my sisters to perform for our parents and their friends. I knew how to do the twist, the swim, and the mashed potato. But this was different. I was about to solo with undivided attention from Michael, the boy I wanted to impress.

My first attempt was hugely awkward. I snapped my fingers, trying to find the rhythm. Mostly, I was worrying about my backside described in the Commodores' song "Brick House." Like her, I was lettin' it all hang out.

Once others started moving down the "Soul Train" line, my self-obsession abated. Susie, an exhibitionist at heart, hammed it up, incorporating modern dance moves and shimmying her shoulders with her eyes closed to, once again, Donna Summer's "Love to Love You Baby"—only this time, she was sober. La Toya seemed more self-conscious than I was and danced stiffly down the line the first few times.

Of course, Michael's move was the most fluid and easy to follow; he conjured a simple routine with just a few basic steps to remember. At one point I thought he might be using moves from *The Wizard of Oz*—so when he suddenly hooked my arm and led me in a Dorothy-and-Scarecrow romp around the dining room table, my suspicions were confirmed.

When the dance line ended, we moved on to a game Michael and I played often together, called "Dictionary." We pulled out an oversized twenty-five-pound hardcover Webster's Dictionary and one of us opened a random page and selected a word; then the rest of us took turns guessing at the meaning. The person who'd selected the word decided whose answer was the closest to the real thing, then turned the dictionary over to them. The dictionary was so heavy, we decided to keep it on the couch and move our seats accordingly.

The game went on for hours, until we finally admitted it was almost time to say good night.

Before leaving, Michael asked to see my room. I took him back to my small, shared bedroom. He went to the bookshelf and began pulling books down, scanning the titles.

I was still an avid reader and had in recent years become a fan of Pearl S. Buck books, which mostly took place in Asia. I'd developed mad crushes on the characters, and for a while I'd become resolved to only marry someone Japanese or Chinese. Then I read all of Chaim Potok's books, whose main character was a Hasidic Jewish teenager named Asher Lev who was torn between his devotion to his Torah studies and his desire to be a normal teen. Suddenly, Buck's characters no longer interested me as much; Asher became my future fantasy husband. But lately Michael was crowding my fictional crushes out of the competition.

I watched as he touched the copy of *Encyclopedia of Child Care* he'd gifted me, sitting prominently on the shelf, and smiled his sweet smile. I wished he didn't have to leave.

Susie was talking to La Toya when we came out. "Yes, I'll come back. In fact, I plan on attending the meeting on Sunday. I promise."

"That's great, Susie," Michael said. "We really miss you, and we need to stay prepared. Armageddon is almost here."

And with that, it was time to bring the Jacksons home. La Toya, Michael, and Randy piled back into my little car, and I drove the few miles down Ventura Boulevard to drop them off at home. On the way, we talked briefly about the success of our ploy. Both Michael and La Toya thought it had gone well.

This was the kind of good, clean fun Susie needed, they said, to find her way back.

When I got home, Susie was standing in the bedroom with only a bra on, holding fruit up to her chest.

"More like this?" she asked, lifting a tangerine. "Or more like this?" she said holding a grapefruit.

Ignoring her, I plopped down on my bed and opened my diary to a new page.

FORNICATION

That next Sunday, Susie didn't come to the Kingdom Hall as promised.

My mother had connected her with casting calls and photography events to begin building her modeling portfolio. Susie's networking led to a slew of party invitations, and at one of them a Playboy representative handed her a card and asked her to take some test shots. The Playboy opportunity made her obsessed with getting breast implants before the scheduled meeting could take place, and she'd made it happen by borrowing the money.

At the beginning of the meeting, Brother Fleming asked me about her.

"She said she was coming to a meeting, but I don't know for sure when it will be," I answered, but deep inside I already knew she wasn't coming back.

"I understand this might be tricky for you, Darls," he said. "Let me know if you'd like some counseling around how to handle this situation."

Okay, I thought, *this is officially a "situation."*

The same week that Susie had her breast augmentation done, I was called aside by the Elders after a Wednesday night book study to meet in the private chambers at the back of the Kingdom Hall.

Brother Long escorted me to the room, which was marked PRIVATE. When he opened the door there were two Elders already seated inside with an open Bible on the table in front of them.

"It has come to our attention that your sister has been influenced by Satan," Brother Long said, "and we need your help to make things right with Jehovah."

They took turns speaking and asked me to consider how it might have felt for Jesus when others called his friend Mary Magdalene a temptress and a harlot. *Jesus was trying to help her*, they explained, *and we are trying to help your sister.*

Brother Long pointed to the open Bible. "Will you read from the book of Matthew for us, Darls?" As he pushed the Bible in front of me, his face drew so close that I could smell his foul, stale breath. His fleshy finger, with its dirty fingernail, pointed to Chapter 18: Verse 7.

I read it out loud: *"Woe to the world for temptations to sin, for it is necessary that temptations come, but woe to the one by whom the temptations come."*

He quickly turned the onion-skin paper and pointed to Chapter 26: Verse 41.

"The spirit is indeed willing, but the flesh is weak," I read dutifully.

A fifteen-minute interrogation about my sister's sexual conduct ensued.

"Is your sister still a virgin? Has she fornicated?"

"I don't know," I said. I wasn't lying, exactly; I didn't know for sure. But I knew she'd been spending the night with her new boyfriend, so it was likely they'd had sex.

"Darls," Brother Long pressed, "it is your duty to Jehovah to disclose what you know, because lying to an Elder is like lying to Jehovah."

"But I can't know," I insisted. "I wasn't with her, and she hasn't told me anything."

"But you do admit she has a *worldly* boyfriend?"

"Yes," I said, lowering my head and twirling my bookbag handle in my lap.

"Does she sleep over at his house?" another Elder asked.

"I don't know if they sleep—they go to dance events and late-night movies," I said.

"You aren't denying your sister has committed an act of fornication?"

I kept my head lowered.

"You're excused," Brother Long finally said.

I left the room as quickly as I possibly could.

I went straight from the Kingdom Hall to meet La Toya at Four'n Twenty Pies. I found her working on her second piece of lemon meringue pie, with all the white fluffy meringue part pushed to the side.

"They asked if she had a boyfriend," I said, "and if she was fornicating."

"What did you say?" she asked.

"I tried every which way to avoid answering and said things like 'I'm not sure' or 'I don't have proof,' but they reminded me that if I lied to them, I was lying to Jehovah."

La Toya was silent for a while and thoughtfully picked at her pie with a fork. Finally, she said, "I don't know what Susie's thinking. How could she do this now, when the end is so near? I feel so bad for you, Darls. I think she'll realize eventually that the worldly life is not for her. Oh, this is all so awful."

I thought about the word "fornication." I'd never heard it before becoming a Jehovah's Witness. It was such a strange and cold word. It sounded worse to me than the curse word for sex.

I wanted to talk to Susie about what had just happened. I hoped it would help her see that the Elders were worried about her. But it seemed more likely that she would see this as just another reason to leave the religion.

I spent a long time thinking about the most diplomatic way to tell her—but I didn't get the opportunity until it was too late.

The following Sunday at the end of the meeting Brother Long announced from the podium in front of a packed Kingdom Hall: "Susan Centola has been *disfellowshipped* for conduct unbecoming a Christian."

Glancing around, my eyes met Rosalie's first. She looked smug.

I looked over at Michael, who wiped away a tear and subtly blew me a kiss with one finger from across the room.

Afterward, I sat in my pew paralyzed, waiting for the others to leave their seats. La Toya, Michael, and Katherine surrounded me, and Katherine took my hand. She wiped her eyes with a tissue and handed one to me.

"Let's all go to lunch," she suggested. "How about Ah Fongs for Chinese?"

I nodded mutely and we headed down the aisle together. Walking out of the Kingdom Hall, I felt so thankful for their support. No one else said a word to me as we shuffled out of the building, but the looks and stares coming my way were a mixture of pity and contempt. I felt somehow tainted.

Outside the door, Brother Long was standing in position, like he was waiting for me.

"Pardon me, Sister Jackson, I'll only steal Sister Centola for a moment," he said.

"I'll meet you at the car," I told them.

The Elder informed me that it was important for me to consider my relationship with my sister in a new way, to demonstrate my loyalty to Jehovah. "Failure to comply by associating with your sister is equal to rejecting the laws of Jesus and Jehovah," he warned.

"Okay, but what does that mean, exactly?" I asked. "We live together."

"You must refrain from speaking to her about anything other than what is absolutely necessary to conduct family business," he said.

That sounded not only impossible but ridiculous. *We share a bedroom*, I thought.

He warned me that I could put the congregation at risk if I failed to follow the rules—that I must protect not only myself but also my fellow members from moral and spiritual contamination.

"Please come to me or any of the Elders for guidance," he said, "as we are here to help you through this difficult time with your unrepentant sister."

Unrepentant. I repeated the word in my mind as I made my way to the parking lot.

Michael was in the back seat of the red Mercedes sedan, and he opened the car door as I approached. He immediately started making jokes, pretending to order the food we would be eating for lunch with a Chinese accent.

"Oh, Michael, you're so silly," Katherine said, giggling.

La Toya criticized his accent, saying she thought it sounded more like a cartoon character than a real person.

"That's right, Toya, I am a cartoon character," he quipped. "So, thank you for the compliment."

I was grateful for the laugh.

When we got to the restaurant, I told the Jacksons what Brother Long had told me.

"How are you supposed to avoid speaking with your sister?" Michael said, shaking his head. He added that perhaps it was meant to motivate the disfellowshipped person to come back into the fold, because they'd miss their relationships with their friends and family.

While I appreciated Michael's perspective, that sounded like emotional blackmail to me.

Katherine said she would speak with her daughter Rebbie's husband, the Elder at a Kingdom Hall in Kentucky.

Then we enjoyed our lunch and the conversation moved on from Susie.

When I got home, my mother was in the kitchen making a pot roast for dinner. "Susie has some big news," she said excitedly.

I opened the fridge and pulled out a carton of orange juice. I glanced over at my mother as I poured myself a glass.

"Your sister is moving into the Playboy Mansion for a few months," she announced, beaming. "Hugh Hefner invited her himself. I'm driving her there next week and I was also asked to attend Movie Night with her."

"Wow," was all I could muster.

At least I wouldn't have to navigate not speaking to my sister who slept three feet away from me. I didn't think I would have been able to uphold the expectation to shun her. Still, it was disconcerting that my mother was so nonchalant about her young, naïve daughter not only posing for *Playboy* magazine but also living in the Playboy Mansion.

There was so much for me to ponder, on top of the loss I felt knowing my sister would not endure the upcoming tribulation, the war of Armageddon. *If I survive*, I thought, *I'll be sentenced to eternal life without anyone from my family.* How could I feel excited about my future?

I had held out hope that my family would one day hear the message and convert, but this seemed even less likely now. In a way, I envied Susie for no longer believing in The

Truth. She no longer had to struggle with living a life of rigidity and rules. She was free to be an eighteen-year-old.

Susie, for her part, didn't seem to feel any remorse or regret. She was so kind to me when I told her about my meeting with the Elders and how they'd asked me if she was still a virgin. She said she forgave me because I was cornered by authority figures, and that she understood that while I couldn't lie, I also didn't directly answer their questions.

She knew the consequences of lying.

"It's pretty great being able to tell a lie without being afraid of what will happen to you after you die," she bragged, then cocked her head and studied me closely. "Would you ever consider leaving the religion, Darls?"

My mouth said no, but in my heart, I felt, for the first time perhaps, an immense *maybe*.

Having transitioned from a small private school, I felt intimidated by my large public university, and socially unprepared to be a college freshman. I did finally feel intellectually challenged, though—so unlike my years at Cal Prep, where it had been easy for me to make the honor roll for four consecutive years and advance two years ahead of my grade.

The library on campus was four stories high and I spent many hours there between classes, sitting at a desk with a bronze and green glass lamp, enclosed in the privacy of my own cubicle. I found refuge in the familiar world of books, sitting on a library stool for hours on end, combing through books with a thirst for knowledge. I was drawn to the comparative religion section of the stacks.

I came across the book *30 Years a Watchtower Slave*, written by a disfellowshipped (and disgruntled) ex-Jehovah's Witness, but was too frightened to even touch the binding. I reached for it several times but always stopped myself in fear of betraying Jehovah, knowing this book was prohibited reading. I pictured the Wicked Witch from *The Wizard of Oz*, her hand recoiling from the ruby slippers even as she reached for them. Apostate literature was the work of Satan; but I had to admit I was curious.

I was fascinated by the vast range of religions that existed in the world and by the rich history of theology. I learned that many spiritual belief systems originated for political reasons only to become a set of convoluted doctrines followed by millions. I was surprised by the infancy of Jehovah's Witnesses—it was so new, less than a hundred years old—and I was particularly struck by the fact it was founded by a single man.

It was in that university library where the seeds of doubt truly began to grow, leading me to begin questioning the rigidity of The Truth.

It was slow and incremental. I compartmentalized it and continued to be both a university student and a student of Jehovah. In one book, Jehovah's Witnesses was referred to as a cult and reading that took my breath away. I learned the term implied an element of "brainwashing" and tried to brush away the next logical thought: that I might be brainwashed.

Jehovah's Witnesses fulfilled some of the other signature traits of a cult, such as creating an elitist status among members by discouraging association with non-members. I learned that cults were usually shame-based, used peer pressure to control thinking and behavior, and discouraged higher education to maintain ignorance.

As I made one connection after another between Jehovah's Witnesses and cults, my neat and tidy spiritual world began to unravel.

One evening in December, Mitch Smith came over for dinner.

Mitch was the adult son of one of my mother's lifelong friends; he was an intellectual, very well-read, and a classically trained actor and singer. At family gatherings, he often debated religion with me, which usually ended with him saying he wanted to tear his hair out with frustration over my blind devotion to Jehovah's Witnesses. I thought he secretly enjoyed the discourse, though, and figured he was eager to remind me that 1975 was soon ending and there had yet to be a bloody Battle of Armageddon.

Considering how wobbly I was feeling in my convictions, and with Susie's recent disfellowshipping, I hoped to avoid engaging with Mitch about my religion that night.

My mom couldn't help herself, however. "Yep, we're still here, Darlsy," my mother said. "And the idiots you blindly follow will have some rigorous explaining to do soon."

Mitch sensed my internal struggles and took pity on me. "Hey Darls," he said, "I'm going out of town next weekend and I need someone to stay over and watch my cat. Do you think you can help me out?"

I looked at my mother.

She considered the proposal for a moment, then nodded. "Lisa lives right next door, so I think you'll be safe enough."

"I'm working Friday and Saturday night at the movie theater, but my shifts are only about six hours," I said.

Mitch smiled. "That's fine. Thank you for the help!"

I was so excited at the thought of having some real privacy for a change. Next weekend couldn't come soon enough.

Mitch's apartment was filled with books—mostly literature, philosophy, and poetry.

He'd left out a few books and magazine articles about the dangers of cult religions and mind-control techniques, and I suspected he'd done so deliberately. Though I knew I shouldn't read them, I couldn't help myself.

On a book rack in the bathroom, a magazine was left open to a story that was about the practices of a cult known as "The Children of God." I placed it on the bedside table and glanced at it a few times before finally exploring the contents.

My hands trembled as I opened the magazine. Somewhere in my heart, I felt this was going to be a game-changer. I stared at the first page until my eyes blurred the print into a zebra pattern.

What if I read this and don't agree with it? I wondered. *Do I need to confess this act of defiance to an Elder, or will I be considered an unfaithful sinner who doubts the word of God and be doomed to eternal death? What does this mean for my friendship with the Jacksons?*

The other day, I'd told La Toya about the religious studies section of the library and how much information was available regarding the history of Christianity. I was fascinated by the fact that less than 50 percent of the world's population was Christian, with religions like Islam, Buddhism, and Hinduism occupying a significant percentage. I mentioned the idea of exclusivity and how each person believes their faith is the one and only.

"Darls, you know we are in The Truth," she'd insisted. "There's so much evidence to back it up, and the predictions in the New Testament are coming true every day. The signs of the end of the world are so obvious. How could you question it?"

I didn't know how to get her to hear me, and I worried she'd convey my doubts to Michael—or, worse, question whether I was suited to be teaching him the Bible. I found that whenever I voiced any critical thinking about the religion, she became dismissive. I knew I was on a slippery slope. And, of course, what was most difficult about my straying heart was the betrayal of Michael it represented.

What's he supposed to do when the person he counts on for spiritual guidance gets totally derailed? I wondered.

I was in a bind. I couldn't move forward as an authentic mentor when saddled with doubts and questions. And whatever move I might make away from the faith would be a choice to let go of Michael. The solitude in Mitch's apartment made me feel like an adult, with adult longings. How was I supposed to wait for marriage before I explored my sexuality. I wanted to do more than just hold hands while skating or touch arms at the movies—I wanted to kiss him and have him put his arm around me while we walked to lunch. I couldn't believe Michael's father was convinced we were on a path heading down the aisle together when we had the romantic interactions of second graders.

I'd enrolled in a human sexuality course at school—another taboo, according to the standards of the governing body of Elders, but this course had been selected by my college advisor. The class presented the biological development of sexuality, not as a moral issue but as a science with social implications. The topic of masturbation had been introduced with no suggestion of impurity; in fact, my professor described it as a normal human function. Much different from how Jehovah's Witnesses spoke of it, as strictly forbidden.

I was so confused.

The relevant information available in college was likely why the Watchtower Society forbade education. I couldn't stop thinking about the primary criteria that made a religion a cult: forbidding access to factual knowledge.

In my most recent Bible study with Michael, we talked about my decision to move forward with my education. I didn't want Michael to become discouraged by my questioning, so I made the decision to keep much of it to myself. Michael was so devoted to The Truth; he continued to find a way to keep it a priority. He was even talking about getting baptized in the summer. Plus, he had his own pressures—his celebrity was growing—and I didn't want to add to his stress.

I had a Watchtower article from 1969 given to me by an Elder. I read it aloud to Michael:

> *Many schools now have student counselors who encourage one to pursue higher education after high school, to pursue a career with a future in this system of things. Do not be influenced by them. Do not let them brainwash you with the Devil's propaganda to get ahead, to make something of yourself in this world. This world has very little time left... make pioneer service, the full-time ministry, with the possibility of Bethel or missionary service your goal.*

"D, this is just like us being told not to listen to worldly music, but I don't really have a choice in that matter; I make music and that's my life," he said. "You don't have a choice either—what else would you do at sixteen if you didn't go to school? But it's still important to keep up with our Bible studies and watch out for getting discouraged or tempted in any way by Satan."

Recalling his words now, in Mitch's apartment, reading about the Children of God felt reckless somehow. I felt like I was cheating on Michael.

I put the article down and decided to sleep on it.

That night, I had a terrible nightmare. I was locked in the trunk of my car. La Toya was driving, and I could hear Michael asking for me.

"I'm in here, in the trunk," I cried. "Pull over and open the trunk!"

But they couldn't hear me.

When I woke up, I understood that something was changing. I didn't know how long I was going to be able to hide my feelings about Jehovah's Witnesses.

As these thoughts raced through my mind, the apartment phone rang. It was La Toya.

"Are you going to the meeting tonight?" she asked. "I'm presenting a talk, and I'm nervous about it. I was hoping we could meet up beforehand and go over it."

I hadn't planned on going. Michael was out of town, and I wanted to enjoy my time in this newfound, sacred solitude. But I couldn't say no to La Toya if she needed me. "Of course I'll help you," I said.

"How is it being there in that apartment?" she asked. "Are you scared?"

"Yes," I admitted, then told her about my scary dream, but not in detail. If she only knew how fearful I was of being alone—not during this time in the apartment, but for the rest of my life.

Later that afternoon, we met at Carl's Jr.

La Toya was so nervous as she practiced her talk, the pages in her hands rattled while she spoke.

"Darls, this topic is very important for us because it deals with the temptations we face as teenagers," she said. "We need to be on top of it or things could go terribly wrong. What do you think of this scripture from Matthew as a way of beginning?"

I was no longer able to focus as she spoke about warding off the ways of Satan through active prayer. I didn't know how I would get through the meeting.

"La Toya, I'm coming to hear your talk, but then leaving early," I said. "I have a paper due tomorrow, and I need to get home. I'll be up all night as it is."

It was becoming easier and easier to lie.

I read the article about the Children of God that night when I got back to the apartment.

The adjustment to Susie's disfellowshipping took a while. It was strange being on my own at the Kingdom Hall. In some ways it was better for me; her behavior was no longer under scrutiny, and it took some pressure off my need to protect her. On the other hand, it was lonely.

The Jacksons rallied around me, however, and they were so loving and supportive—always saving a seat next to them at meetings and inviting me for meals afterward.

During a November meeting on a Sunday morning, the Elder Fleming gave the main talk from the podium.

The topic was, "How Are You Using Your Life?" The subject matter dealt with how to utilize our precious, limited time in this Old System as we prepared for the New System. The topic struck a chord with all of us. The literature often pointed to autumn 1975 as the date of Armageddon, but that season had already passed.

Fleming gave examples of devoted fellow Witnesses who'd given up their jobs and were living off their pensions and savings so they could contribute more time and effort toward converting people before Armageddon. Savings would not be needed to secure a financial future, since the future was eternal, and we'd all be working for Jehovah.

Michael and I had agreed this talk would contain important information, and as Fleming spoke both of us listened intently. I felt uneasy as the Elder strongly encouraged us all to spread the word of Jehovah. Balancing a job and a full university course load was already overwhelming.

For the last four years, I couldn't have imagined giving anything less than 100 percent devotion. The Truth had always been the truth. But now, it was more and more challenging for me to stay enthusiastic about my religion.

I still felt tremendous guilt over having read the Children of God article, which was compounded by the fact that they had similar beliefs about an expected apocalypse.

I was making a concerted effort to stay the course—I prayed to Jehovah to cleanse my impure thoughts questioning the validity of The Truth. I'd asked Tina and Phil about feeling discouraged, and they'd said Susie getting disfellowshipped represented an opportunity for Satan to enter and create doubt.

That made sense to me. I was being tested, and I wanted to pass.

After the meeting, Michael and I moved toward the front of the Kingdom Hall.

"That talk was so good, D, don't you think?"

His eyes were sparkling with the "God feeling" that I was so desperately trying to revive.

Just as I was about to respond, Fleming stepped off the stage and approached us. His wife, Patience, appeared as well.

"Such an inspiring talk, honey!" she said, giving him a hug.

After a few moments of casual chit-chat, they asked both of us to their house for dinner the following weekend.

"I need to check and see if I'm working," Michael responded kindly. "But I'll call Darls tonight once I know for sure."

"Sounds good to me," I agreed. "Will anyone else be coming to dinner?"

"No, it'll just be the four of us," Elder Fleming said.

I was flattered to be asked, given the exclusive nature of the invite. But also had the suspicion that Elder Fleming was only interested in socializing with me to access Michael.

When Michael and I arrived together at the Flemings' little bungalow house in the northwest Valley, Michael made a joke about holding a *Watchtower Magazine*, as if we were doing our door-to-door service, but I could see he was a bit tense—clenching his hands and then putting them in his back pocket and then clenching them again.

Patience answered the door. She looked like a 1950s housewife, with her neatly curled bangs, modest gingham top, beige knee-length skirt, and matching headband.

She served a dinner of meatloaf, roasted red potatoes, salad with croutons, and string bean casserole with little fried onions from a can over what tasted like Campbell's

Cream of Mushroom Soup. I noticed how passive she was throughout dinner, allowing her husband to dominate the conversation, and speaking only when directly addressed.

"Michael," Fleming asked, "do you get tired of performing the same songs over and over again?"

"Never," he answered.

"Does it get annoying to deal with all the screaming from the fans?"

"No, I never get tired of the fans," Michael answered. "I love my fans."

Another annoying question, I thought. *This is unfair to Michael.* And yet he handled it with such grace.

After a long silence, I interjected, trying to steer the conversation in another direction. "What are the steps you took to become an Elder?" I asked.

Fleming ignored me and proceeded to pose more obvious questions to Michael.

By the end of dinner, I suspected that I was being observed by the Body of Elders because of two converging concerns: my proximity to my recently disfellowshipped, Playboy-affiliated sister, who made me susceptible to corruption, and my influence over Michael, who was viewed as a precious commodity.

As Patience went to get dessert, I couldn't help wondering how they had sex—with the colostomy bag and all.

CHANGE OF COURSE

It was getting more difficult to be a Jehovah's Witness on a college campus, where the concept of critical thinking was highly valued and brought up repeatedly in all my courses. By the second semester of my freshman year, I had begun to embrace the concept as well and was enjoying the freedom of considering multiple points of view and formulating my own perspective. I made an unconscious decision to separate my college experience from my life as a Jehovah's Witness, because they were so incompatible. The religion was a closed system, discouraging innovative and individual thinking. I had never questioned the idea of *not* questioning—until now.

I thought about what my mother had said for years: "Those religious freaks won't allow you to think for yourself."

I was also reminded of what Mrs. Yardum said about cults not allowing "outside" thinking. I hadn't grasped before that she was referring to critical thinking. When witnessing, we often asked our prospective converts to "please have an open mind." Meanwhile, as an already converted

Witness, I had barely grasped even the basic principles of open-mindedness.

La Toya kept asking to visit me at college. I wasn't sure what the appeal was for her. Maybe she was a little envious of me for having a legitimate adult experience in the real world? Though she had traveled all over and been exposed to much more than I had, she seemed to live in a protected world, sheltered by the rigidity of the Jehovah's Witnesses and the extreme privacy of her family. "Darls, can I visit your Song and Sign class tomorrow?" she said. "Do you think that would be okay?"

"Sure," I said—then quickly realized this meant I needed to make a confession. I took a deep breath and exhaled slowly. "Toya, there's something I need to tell you. I participate in Christmas carols in my sign language class, and you'll see my hands moving to the off-limits pagan songs. It's part of my classwork, and I decided not to be a conscientious objector."

Testing the limits with La Toya was a way of preparing myself for the larger test I suspected was coming.

"Darls, Michael has to sing Happy Birthday to people all the time and he did a Christmas album with my brothers, so believe me, I understand," she said without missing a beat. "Sometimes you have to do what you have to do."

While selecting classes for my second semester at University, I was drawn to the Religious Studies registration table. The courses sounded fascinating and there were so many to choose from. I saw the phrase "religious scholar" on much of the material, and that piqued my curiosity. In The Truth, we were taught that members of the Watchtower Society were biblical scholars with a direct connection to Jehovah. Realizing that different Bible interpretations had existed over hundreds of years stimulated my interest.

I stood there for a few minutes, reviewing the syllabi and course descriptions, marveling over all the choices. I had lived in The Truth for the last four years, yet as I hesitated at the registration table, I realized that a part of me must still be seeking the truth.

I walked away and said a silent prayer to Jehovah, and asked for guidance, strength, and direction. I landed in the Special Education section next, where I signed up for two Sign Language courses. I also signed up for Drama and a singing class.

I had been put on academic probation after my first semester, which was an odd experience for me after having only ever earned straight A's. I'd been so certain Armageddon was coming that I'd failed to withdraw from a Western Civilization class before the deadline and saw no need to follow the university's policies and procedures. It had just turned 1976 and since I was still alive, I decided to re-prioritize my grade point average, so I signed up to repeat Western Civilization and take a Mass Communications class—but I still needed one more class for a full course load.

I circled back to the Religious Studies table.

"Hello . . . Darling? Is that how you say your name?" the student representative asked.

"No, it's Darls, pronounced like Charles." I was used to correcting my name.

"Are you interested in Religious Studies?"

"Yes, I am," I admitted. I noticed she had a copy of a book I was in the middle of reading: *The Dove*, by Robin Lee Graham. It was the true story of a sixteen-year-old boy who sailed around the world alone, departing from Southern California. He met his future wife along the way, and she joined him at various international ports during his three-year journey. *National Geographic* had featured his story recently; in fact, I'd just read the article about him that week. He lived with the courage I craved; I, too, longed to follow my dream and travel the world.

"I'm reading that book," I said. "Did you see the film? I've gone to see it at least five times."

"Oh yeah," she said, lighting up. "It was so inspiring!"

We talked about the film and I hung around her table, revisiting the course list. I wanted so badly to take one of the classes—but signing up for one would be crossing a line, and I'd already crossed so many lately.

While waiting for my new acquaintance to finish speaking to another prospective student, I picked up her copy of *The Dove*, opened the cover, and found an inscription:

> *When you can't change the direction of the wind, adjust your sails.*
>
> *Love, Mom*

The message spoke to me and was just the sign I needed to move forward.

I put down the book and registered for a class.

PLAYBOY MANSION

The Jehovah's Witness saying, *Stay Alive 'til 75*, had lost all meaning.

The end of the year, with no Armageddon, was perplexing to many Jehovah's Witnesses. I reviewed something I'd written down from a recent Assembly talk:

> *Many of us have suffered misery, sickness and death. You don't have to experience that anymore. The new order is near... Sell your house, sell everything you own and say, oh boy, how long can I carry on with my private means. That long? Get rid of things! Pioneer! Plan to shower people with magazines during these last few months of this dying system of things!*

I had believed Armageddon was coming with all my heart—and now I needed to recalibrate. The subject was addressed in many subsequent meetings, with the sentiment being that we need to be even more prepared, because now the end could come at any time.

We believed that 6,000 years of human existence would come to an end while an anointed 144,000 Jehovah's

Witnesses who had lived in 1914 were still living. The year 1914 held significant meaning to the Jehovah's Witness interpretation of the Bible and the chronology that led toward Armageddon. This was based on a scripture from Revelations. We had a special celebration every spring to celebrate the few individuals remaining on earth. The 144,000 special ones were supposedly going to heaven and would not be among those of us granted eternal life on earth. There were two or three elderly "anointed ones," or members of the sacred 144,000, in our congregation. I wondered how they knew they were chosen; when I asked, I was told that it was a covenant from Jehovah.

I didn't know what to think.

I approached the tall iron gates of the Playboy Mansion in my beat-up Toyota. An attractive young man with an effeminate voice asked my name and the nature of my visit.

"My name is Darls Centola. My sister, Susie Centola, is staying here," I said. "I'm dropping off a suitcase for her."

He consulted his clipboard.

"Ah, yes, I see you're expected. Go down the main driveway and park against the white fence behind the fountain. I'll let Miss Susie know you have arrived."

Wow, so formal, I thought. Like the Jackson home, the driveway stretched far back, but the mansion at the end of this driveway made the Jackson home seem like a cottage. The estate was as long as a city block, with numerous floors, high windows, and at least five chimneys sticking out of the massive rooftop. Rolls-Royces, Corvettes, and black stretch limousines crowded the massive circular driveway.

Susie came to greet me. She was wearing denim hot pants and a wafer-thin, midriff-baring Playboy T-shirt with the iconic bunny logo on the front. She wasn't wearing a bra; her legs were brown and toned. It had only been two weeks since I'd last seen her, and she seemed so different.

"C'mon," she said, "I'll give you a tour. My studio is in the grotto, behind the pool house."

We walked past the massive swimming pool, where a few perfectly shaped women in skimpy bikinis were either lounging on deck chairs or floating in the water. One long-legged blonde on a raft was topless and it was difficult not to stare at her large, unnatural-looking breasts.

Butlers dressed in white suits served beverages and food on silver trays, making the Mansion seem more like a resort than a residence.

Oddly enough, I was a big fan of *Playboy* magazine's in-depth interviews. My parents subscribed and in our liberal household the magazine was seen as a cultural and political publication. I felt wicked for reading it, however, and had never disclosed it to any of my Jehovah's Witness associates.

Susie led me off to the side of the pool into a shadowy area with green and red flood lights reflecting off wet rock walls. Water flowed into hot tubs below and a series of grottos that looked like man-made caves with separate pools. They were all unoccupied.

I inhaled the musty dampness of this indoor water playground. "Why are there so many separate areas and why are they empty?" My question echoed off the walls.

"They get filled up at night," Susie said as she swung open a heavy wooden door.

She ushered me into the room, in the middle of which sat a strange chair.

"Do you know what that is, Darls?"

"No," I admitted, "but it looks like a twisted version of a chair from the dentist's office."

"It's a fucking chair," she said, nonchalantly.

It took a few beats for me to catch that.

"You mean 'fucking' as in 'goddamn chair,' or it's used for...?" I paused. I was not supposed to curse, much less speak to my disfellowshipped sister about topics deemed unnecessary.

"It's for having sex and they call it the *fucking chair*," Susie clarified.

My mind was blown. I slowly circled the contorted chair, trying to make sense of it.

I didn't quite get it. There were lots of padded red leather pieces and thick metal components wrapped with cloth. It was heavy and large and had places to put your feet, but they were facing the wrong way.

"Sit in it." My sister pushed me toward the chair.

I hesitated and then climbed up.

"It's meant for a variety of sexual positions."

I wasn't sure exactly what that meant but I slid quickly out of the chair and continued to examine it. *This is so weird*, I thought.

"Susie, I'm worried about you," I said after regaining my composure. "What about our beliefs? What about Armageddon?"

"Really, Darls." She rolled her eyes. "It was supposed to be the end of the world last year and now it's 1976. I don't believe it anymore. You—or, rather, *we*—were brainwashed. Don't you think it's weird to expect everyone in the world to perish at the hands of a loving God just because people don't convert?"

This was a valid question, but I knew my sister. The religion's limits on personal freedom was far more likely behind her decision to leave the faith. I felt afraid for her—afraid of the road she was going down. It was a big leap to go from the Kingdom Hall to the halls of the Playboy Mansion. How could she agree to be photographed naked for the whole world to see?

"Susie, how could you even ask me that? You know the consequences of rejecting Jehovah," I pressed. "What about everything you know about the great tribulation?"

"I don't want to discuss that anymore," she said firmly. "There's so much to tell you."

Susie had just returned from Santa Cruz; she was enrolled for a semester at UC Santa Cruz, but left after three weeks. That's when Hugh Hefner invited her to stay at the Mansion to finish her centerfold photo shoot.

"Guess who followed me up to Santa Cruz?" she prompted me, grinning.

I couldn't guess. I was so nervous about being here and still feeling uncomfortable about the chair. I wondered if Susie ever tried it but didn't dare ask.

"Shel Silverstein!" she blurted. "He met me at movie night at Hef's and we stayed in touch afterward. He surprised me and showed up on campus."

I thought about how I'd given his children's book, *The Giving Tree*, as a gift to Michael.

"All the girls at Santa Cruz were so jealous, I had to get out of there." She tossed her hair. "I don't think college is for me right now. When I flew into LAX, a driver was waiting for me with a sign that had my name on it and then he drove me here in a limousine."

"What happened with Shel Silverstein?" I asked.

She ignored me and changed the subject to other celebrities, including Warren Beatty and Bill Cosby.

"Yeah, Darls, Warren is so sweet," she gushed. "He takes me and this other centerfold friend of mine out for nice dinners and we have so much fun. People stare at me like I'm a movie star."

I knew she was a goner. There was no way she could be enticed back into the world of knee-length skirts and meetings at the Kingdom Hall three times a week.

I drove away from the Playboy Mansion feeling like I'd just committed a sin.

TAP DANCING

Michael got baptized that summer at an Assembly, and I knew he'd no longer need me as much after that. I was losing my grip on the religion just as he was getting more involved. A ripple of sadness ran through me. Our solidarity in The Truth was dissipating.

Michael and La Toya were preparing to perform in an upcoming television program called *The Jackson Family Variety Show*. We were hanging out in their music studio, where they had a portable vinyl tap floor, and taking turns—or, rather, they were taking turns while I watched—trying out dance moves.

La Toya had been more focused on performing since the Vegas act, and I enjoyed seeing her passion. So, when she'd invited me to practice with them, I'd been happy to come.

"Toya, try this." Michael did some fast fancy footwork.

"You're showing off, Michael," La Toya said, giggling—and then impressed me with her ability to repeat Michael's moves.

I applauded, and then Michael gave La Toya some notes about her footing and where to put her weight.

"You know you should never talk to a girl about her weight," she joked.

I felt so close to my friends and, at the same time, incredibly alone. I needed to talk to someone about my ever-increasing doubts.

I decided to get in touch with Ken Lewis, who had been disfellowshipped a year earlier. I had admired the way he carried himself and his keen intellect. He also had a younger brother who was still a Witness, so our circumstances were similar.

I looked Ken up in the phone book and dialed his number. Much to my surprise, he picked up on the first ring.

"Hi, Ken," I began. "I'm not sure if you remember me. This is Darls . . . from the Sherman Oaks congregation."

There was a long pause . . . then: "Hi, Darls. Of course I remember you. Did you get disfellowshipped? I heard about Susie."

I understood why he would ask me that question; after all, it was forbidden for me to speak to him if I was still a member of the religion. "I am . . . struggling with my beliefs," I admitted. "Sometimes I know for sure I'm in The Truth, and other times it seems as though it can't be right."

"I totally understand," he said. "What do you think you're going to do?"

That was a huge question, and one I didn't have an answer for.

"Do you think we could get together and talk?" I asked.

We arranged to meet within the next few days.

Two days later, I went to the Jacksons' house for a Bible study. I felt like a liar and a bad person for having dissenting thoughts.

I parked my Toyota in the circular driveway next to a shiny gold Rolls-Royce and two high-end Mercedes-Benzes. I walked along the path and saw a golden glow emanating from Michael's bedroom window.

The blue light shining from the large TV in the family room also noticeably brightened as I headed toward the sliding glass doors.

At that moment, for reasons I can't fully understand, I realized that I disagreed with any belief system that restricted freedom of thinking.

Individual thinking is to be valued and nurtured, not oppressed! I felt this in my bones.

This new awareness was cellular, and my whole being vibrated with the possibility of liberation.

La Toya slid open the glass door and greeted me with a huge smile. It was difficult to look her directly in the eyes. I couldn't understand why I felt like a horrible person if The Truth might not be the truth after all. I knew I shouldn't feel guilty about having legitimate questions.

La Toya and I sat in the Addams Family chairs while we waited for Michael to join us. The three of us were going to have a Bible study together—but this time, for the first time ever, La Toya and Michael would lead the study.

Michael said the article they'd chosen to cover was about teens and the temptations to stray from one's faith.

He looked me deep in the eyes. "It's normal for us to entertain doubts occasionally," he started, "and the most important thing is to share your concerns with others in The Truth, so we can hold each other up and stand strong. "Keep on the watch and pray continually, that you may not enter into temptation," he said, quoting from the Book of Matthew.

What exactly is tempting me? I wondered. *The search for facts?*

I wanted to be my old self, the person without misgivings, but I couldn't any longer—something had irrevocably changed. We took turns reading paragraphs and commenting on the content. I was at a loss for words.

"*The Watchtower* says that this is a test," Michael continued, "and you're being tested because Jehovah knows you're worthy of making this choice. Otherwise, you wouldn't be given the opportunity."

Jehovah's Witnesses believed that the narrative in *The Watchtower* was a direct message from Jehovah to the Governing Body—the corporation that was the Watchtower and Tract Society.

Now I found it hard to swallow that a bunch of old white guys in Brooklyn were sitting around getting special instructions from Jehovah then transcribing it into a magazine. But that was not the case for my friends. Each time La Toya spoke, she'd look at Michael, who'd nod and add his own comment to deepen the point. I noticed he was using the very style I'd used to teach him: he'd summarize the point of a given passage, and then ask a question that demanded a "yes" answer.

Persuasion Techniques 101.

"Don't you agree, Darls, that some will fall away, and that is the work of Satan and his clever temptations?"

I nodded without enthusiasm. Satan seemed like a mythological character to me at this point. The Bible quote indicated that the pull toward anything outside of Jehovah's world was sourced from Satan. That idea just seemed like bad fiction.

Michael earnestly quoted the scriptures and then started pretending to be different nerdy kids drawn to do bad things. His exaggerated performance sent us into fits of laughter. *How could I consider leaving this haven?* I loved my friends for caring about my life and welfare—and just a few months prior, I would've taken their same position. When Ken was disfellowshipped, I believed he'd been led into temptation by Satan. Now, my close friends seemed to be thinking the same of me.

I dreaded what might happen to our connection if I left the religion. These were the people I most admired and counted on for emotional and social support. I also feared them seeing me as "the other," the outlier. But now that I understood how mind control worked—how people followed blindly because it was impossible to break free without condemnation—I realized I would feel alone whether I stayed in the Jehovah's Witnesses or whether I left. The prospect frightened me.

"Do you want to stay for dinner, Darls?" La Toya asked.

"Sorry, I can't . . . I have work," I lied.

I drove straight from the Jacksons' house to an apartment complex in North Hollywood, where I climbed the flight of stairs toward Ken's apartment.

I noticed the difference between how I felt compared to a few hours ago at the Jacksons'. It was as if I were two different people. I was beginning to imagine a future shaped by my own choices.

Then I thought of Michael and La Toya—their earnestness in wanting to keep me in The Truth—and my hope turned to dread. I felt like I was losing my mind.

Ken opened the door. His toothy smile and strong, handsome jawline struck me, and I remembered why Susie had a crush on him. He gave me a big hug and it felt good to be wrapped in his arms. The hold was a bit longer than a normal greeting, and I could sense a sadness in him.

We sat on the sofa in his small apartment. He said he was working as a mechanic, learning how to repair airplane engines.

"I haven't spoken to my family in six months," he shared. "My brother won't respond to my calls or letters." He was fighting back tears. "I wish I knew how my younger sisters were doing. I really miss them."

He stared into space, wiping away sweat beads forming on his brow. I couldn't imagine being ostracized from my entire family.

"Do you ever regret your choice?" I asked.

"No," he answered emphatically. "I didn't really have a choice. I could choose my family over my freedom, I suppose, but I don't respect the Elders, or the religion for that matter. I wish it was different, that I could go along with their beliefs, but I couldn't fake it any longer."

Ken talked about his loneliness and how difficult it was to make new friends.

"I didn't realize my whole world was Jehovah's Witnesses and that I was closed off from the real world," he said. "Sometimes I think my mother would leave if she could, but it's so difficult. Her whole family is in The Truth, and she could never disobey my father." He tilted his head and looked at me. "What is it that changed for you, Darls?"

"Mostly, it's a new understanding I have of religions," I explained. "They're so vast, and there are so many ways to understand God. Going to college really opened my mind. Jehovah's Witnesses discourage individual thinking and that seems so wrong. I learned about this thing called *groupthink*; it's the idea that the consensus thinking of the group overrides individual rational thought and conforming to the group means degrading those that differ. That's what disfellowshipping is. The psychological effects of shunning family members is a powerful strategy to keep people in line with their beliefs."

It felt like I'd finally taken a breath after holding it for too long.

"I can see through it so clearly," I said. Then I looked away. "And yet, at other times, I vacillate and question if I'm making a huge mistake."

"I could never have said that, but it's so true," Ken said compassionately. "I don't have the words you do—you're learning so much at college, Darls. I really get what you're saying."

I liked the compliment, but not nearly as much as the feeling I got from being free to speak my thoughts.

"You're really taking the time to sort this out and make a thoughtful decision about your future. I really respect that," Ken said.

That was comforting, especially since I had a meeting with the Elders coming up and a list of questions ready. I told him about my trepidation, and he said the thought of it made him shudder.

"Darls, what do you think they'll do when you question The Truth?" he asked.

"I just want to understand the things that aren't adding up for me."

"Promise you'll let me know how things go," he said.

"I promise," I said, and gathered myself to go.

He stood and walked me toward the door. We paused there, standing close to one another, and had an awkward moment.

"May I give you a kiss?" Ken asked.

I wasn't sure if he meant a friendly kiss or a *kiss* kiss.

"Okay," I said.

He gently put his mouth on mine. His lips felt so soft. He opened his mouth just a little and looked me in the eyes, then closed his own, breathing me in. It was exhilarating.

I walked down the stairs feeling like a real grown-up. I thought about Michael and wondered what it would be like to kiss *his* lips.

Ken was so encouraging, and just the kind of support I needed to move forward with my quest for the truth about

The Truth. I tried to put Michael out of my mind for now. Otherwise, I knew I'd never leave.

A NEW ELDER IN TOWN

My meeting with the Elders was scheduled to take place after a Sunday talk.

Michael and La Toya's older sister, Rebbie, recently moved from Kentucky to Los Angeles with her family. Her husband, Nathaniel, was assigned as an Elder to our congregation.

The Jacksons were excited, and the entire congregation turned out to welcome our new members. Katherine beamed with pride that day at the Kingdom Hall. Rebbie was super tiny and pretty like La Toya and all together they seemed like such a tight-knit family. I wondered if I should stick around and become part of this happy reunion.

I asked myself the same question I'd been repeating all morning: *Are you sure you want to make this big decision, Darls?*

The only answer I heard was: *Wait until after the meeting with the Elders.*

I had to wait extra-long after the meeting ended; welcoming the new Elder and his family was taking a while. I stood with Michael in the back of the Kingdom Hall.

"D, allow your mind to be open to what the Elders advise," he said. "Remember, this doubt is only a temporary feeling, and it will pass."

"I know, Michael. I will."

I felt the familiar pang of disloyalty because of my desire to have an open mind—but as I defined it, not the Church. My stress was compounded by now knowing the religion I followed with devotion was a barrier to me being my authentic self.

La Toya joined us and tried to engage me in our usual schtick—commenting, making a joke, and then riffing.

"You're so silly, Toya. You need to stop playing," Michael said with a forced seriousness. Then he made a funny face.

I was having a hard time joining this lighthearted play, as I was about to enter the lion's den.

Brother Long approached us. "We're ready to see you now, Sister Darls." He pointed toward the office.

I followed behind him, turning my back on my friends.

"Brother Fleming will join us in a moment," Brother Long said as we were seated.

We sat there in awkward silence, broken only by Brother Long belching a few times as he riffled through a few pages in a three-ringed notebook. I could smell his rancid breath from multiple feet away.

"Excuse me," he finally said, not referring to his indigestion. "I'm going to get Brother Fleming."

He left his notebook open. I was tempted to peek inside and see what he'd written, but it was too risky.

By the time the two of them came back, my heart was beating fast, and my palms were sweaty.

"Sister Darls, tell us what's troubling you," they began. "How can we be of service?"

I reached in my purse and removed a piece of folded lined paper, where I had written down a few thoughts and questions.

"We are taught Armageddon won't occur until all of Earth's inhabitants have been given a chance to either accept or reject Jehovah," I began. "The Earth has two and a half billion inhabitants. Some live in remote areas of the Amazon, unseen by other humans. Also, there are orphans on the streets of Mexico. How could they be responsible for knowing whether they accept Jehovah into their lives?"

The Elders opened their well-worn Bibles and started quoting scriptures—ones I knew too well. Their message, as always, instructed me to put my full trust in Jehovah. They also made it clear that I was demonstrating a lack of faith by questioning him.

I had lost my faith. I could no longer follow the simplistic message that demanded blind faith.

Brother Long seemed impatient. He looked at his watch; fat bulged out from under the shiny black band. Brother Fleming, however, didn't stop smiling at me. I'd long respected him, so I was disappointed he wasn't being more helpful.

"Sister Darls, you're such a pretty young lady," Brother Fleming said. "Why are you trying to poke holes in the doctrine? You have always been such a good example of a devoted Christian youth. We understand you're having difficulty because of your sister leaving Jehovah's Witnesses."

She didn't even leave, I thought—*she was disfellowshipped.*

"How are things going at the university?" Brother Long asked abruptly.

I wasn't sure what to make of this turn in conversation. "Fine," I said cautiously.

"I know Tina and Phil being away in Florida has been hard on you as well."

That was true. I missed them and wished they were here to walk me through this minefield.

"How much time do you spend studying with Michael?"

Now this was a question I wasn't expecting.

"I turn in my study hours every week," I said. "It's been a bit less lately since we no longer go to school together, but I go to his house when he's in town—at least once or twice a week. We also talk on the phone about the literature. We average about ten hours per week."

Brother Long exchanged a glance with Brother Fleming and then quickly scribbled something down.

"What other questions did you bring?" Brother Fleming asked in a soft tone.

"Well, if the Jehovah's Witnesses religion is only about a hundred years old, what about all the millions of people who lived on the Earth before it was founded? Will they have an opportunity for eternal life on earth?"

My voice started to shake.

Brother Long breathed a heavy sigh. "We don't question the authority of Jehovah, because we trust in him fully."

"But we were certain Armageddon was to occur in 1975, and people gave up their life savings, and it turned out to be wrong." I looked down at my hands, tensely folded on the table.

"That was merely a suggested date," Brother Long said, "and we've since adjusted to new information from the Watchtower Society."

They revised history! This was in stark contradiction to what I'd heard preached from the podium for years.

We went back and forth for about thirty minutes, but the discourse only seemed to repeat itself.

"I don't have any more questions," I finally said, and rose to go.

I don't know what I was thinking would be different about this inquiry, but my curiosity was turning into disappointment and anger.

DECIDED

That night at dinner, our apartment was stifling hot from the October Santa Ana winds. The temperature was almost unbearable.

"I picked up deli and you can make your own sandwiches," Mom announced. "It's way too hot to turn on the stove."

She was wearing a white halter top and shorts set, and her usual shellacked, piled-high hair had melted and was hanging limp in her face. I was expecting a call from Michael to talk about my meeting with the Elders and wanted to get dinner going, so I made a turkey sandwich and told my brother to get his plate.

Susie was visiting for the evening and telling a story about living at the Mansion; my mother was transfixed. Susie wasn't around much these days, so it was a treat to have her home.

"Bill Cosby asked me out and when I said no, he was so mean about it," she said.

"Really? What did he say?" my mother asked, filling her glass with ice and vodka.

"Can we all sit down and eat?" I pleaded. "I have something important to tell you."

"I'm not ready to eat yet," Mom said. She sat down with her cocktail and lit a cigarette. "What's your big news, Darlsy?"

"I'm thinking of resigning from the religion," I blurted.

"Hallelujah!" Susie smiled, then stood up and did a pirouette.

My mother's reaction was more serious. "Tell us more, Darls."

Who is this woman? She seemed so maternal suddenly. I appreciated that this news was significant to her. It certainly was for me.

"I had a meeting with the Elders today and asked lots of questions about the doctrine."

"Dogma," Mom said.

"Okay, either way." I shrugged. "I left feeling disappointed, and I don't believe it's the truth anymore."

"Do you know what you're going to do?" she asked.

"I'm thinking of writing a letter to the organization and letting them know that I'm withdrawing as a member. Do you think that's a good idea?"

"That's a great idea, and I can help you," she said. "Let's do it tonight."

My mother wrote the best letters. She was gifted at concise and clear communication. I wasn't used to her paying this much positive attention to me. It was refreshing to connect with her after the years of tension around being a Witness.

For all her flaws, my mother was fiercely committed to justice and equality. She was progressive, outspoken, and deeply liberal—vehemently opposed to Nixon, outraged by Watergate, and disgusted by the Vietnam War.

My inner conflict between respecting and fearing my mother was morphing into something more grown-up. Her desire to advocate for me felt loving. But I also wanted this letter to be from *me*, and I wasn't sure she fully understood my dilemma.

She took the lead. "Darls, what's the most important thing you want to convey? We'll build your statement around the significant points and make sure we're firm yet clear about the purpose of the letter."

Susie left the room to talk on the phone. I was relieved, because Michael would call soon; a busy signal would buy me some time.

"What would happen if you didn't write a letter, and you stopped participating?" Mom asked.

"I thought about that," I said, nodding. I explained that if I wasn't completely clear about the reasons for my decision there was a chance I'd be misunderstood—that they'd think I'd done something worthy of disfellowshipping—and then I wouldn't be able to speak with Michael and La Toya.

"Those fucking backwards, medieval morons," Mom said.

"They're creeps!" Susie shouted from the other room.

"As much as I disagree with their interpretation of the Bible," I responded, "I still feel like being a Jehovah's

Witness helped me be a better person, get good grades, and stay away from drugs."

My mother rolled her eyes. "Okay, let's really get across to them that you're resigning—and further, that you're not flexible about it."

"Most people leave because they can't live within the requirements for a pure, clean lifestyle. I'm leaving because I disagree with how they interpret the Bible."

Mom lit a cigarette and inhaled deeply, then blew out a trail of smoke. "Go and get the Selectric typewriter out of my bedroom," she said. "Let's write this letter."

We worked on it for about an hour. Mom's input helped me formulate my own ideas. Tired and eager to talk to Michael since Susie was off the phone, I asked to take a break and come back to the letter. Mom agreed; she and Susie were involved in a miniseries called *Rich Man, Poor Man* and they were eager to watch the next episode.

"By the way," I said, "there's a machine where you can record a TV show and watch it later." I told her about my recent introduction to the Jacksons' Betamax video recorder.

"I'm sure that's for the Rich Man and not the Poor Man like us," she said.

As if on cue, the phone rang.

It was Michael.

TELLING MICHAEL

"How was your meeting with the Elders today?" Michael asked. His voice sounded serious. "Did you get some answers? Are you feeling better about things?"

I wish he would wake up with me, but that seemed too hopeful at this point. The situation couldn't have been trickier. As my Bible student these past years, he was conditioned to view me as an authority, and now my message was in direct conflict with what he knew to be true.

I launched into my arguments against our teachings: "Michael, how could a loving God murder innocent children because their parents don't convert?"

"D, you know we can't pretend to understand the complex mind and heart of Jehovah," he returned. "We are humans and God is perfect."

He used familiar, worn-out Bible quotes centered around belief and faith as the meat of his argument.

"The Governing Body that writes our literature are mere men and they have changed the Bible interpretation numerous times. How can that be blindly trusted? I mean, we were so convinced that Armageddon was going to occur in 1975, right? Our fellow Brothers and Sisters were applauded for spending their savings and devoting themselves to service instead of preparing for their future. I let myself fail a college course because I believed the promise of the End of Times. That is so irresponsible! I can't get my mind to think like that anymore, and I don't know how to change my thinking back to the way it was."

"Darls, if it's not the truth, we'll know it at some point," he said gently.

"What if, for me, that point is now?"

"What if you're wrong?"

"Michael, my head is aching from asking myself that. But I know one thing for sure: I can't believe what I don't believe. That would make me a hypocrite."

"I know, of course you can't," he said, his voice going a little higher.

"I need to tell you something," I said. "I wrote a letter to the governing body, telling them to pull my publishing card."

There was a long silence on the other end of the line—the loudest silence I'd ever experienced.

"Jehovah loves you and so do I," he said finally. "I'll call you tomorrow, D."

Then he hung up the phone.

THE LETTER

October 14, 1976

To the Body of Elders:

This letter is to inform you of my decision to withdraw from the organization of Jehovah's Witnesses.

This decision was not made on impulse. I have come to the realization that it would be hypocritical of me to continue participating since I disagree with the doctrines that are part of Jehovah's Witnesses' interpretation. I trust you will take the necessary steps to notify the society and pull my publisher's card.

It is my firm request you advise the congregation not to call me and attempt to change my decision.

It is important for me to let you know I have not trespassed or committed any sin that would warrant disfellowshipping.

My association has brought many beneficial experiences and I've enjoyed the privilege of meeting so many lovely people.

My formative years prior to my involvement with Witnesses included reason, logic, and love for my fellow man. As I mature, the "truth" becomes the power of our father in all men regardless of the dogma that is perpetuated in various religious sects.

My family and I do practice the two commandments of life from Jesus and therefore we follow religion according to the true law of God.

I am enthusiastic about meeting people of all walks of life and continuing my development as an individual with an open mind.

Respectfully,
Darls Centola

I dropped the envelope in the corner mailbox the following day. There was a shadow of my handprint on the white envelope from my sweaty grip. I felt nauseated and lightheaded. I pictured Michael with a disappointed look on his face, filled with sadness and pity for my being led astray.

It was so clear now: I had been brainwashed all these years, convinced that I was right and those who didn't believe were unenlightened.

A cult's method for creating loyalty is through the control of information and thought, as well as the behavior and emotions of its members. This had been systematically enforced through my experience as a Jehovah's Witness—they controlled information by forbidding me to speak with ex-members, including my own sister, and discouraging my access to non-cult sources of knowledge via the banning of certain books. They divided information into an insider-vs.-outsider doctrine, which is why anything worldly was considered satanic.

Thought control occurred through four meetings a week of repetitive indoctrination, and the rejection of rational analysis and critical thinking (no wonder they prohibited higher education), while behavioral control looked like the restriction of clothing and hairstyles. And nothing could be more emotionally controlling than the two threats that had kept me in line for the last four years: disfellowshipping and Armageddon. I allowed myself to imagine all the freedom coming my way. . . birthdays, holidays, and getting rid of knee-length skirts. But the most important was living according to my own truth, not what authority figures told me. This was what I'd been wanting. Yet, no matter how I tried to console myself, it was agonizing.

SPIRITUAL ABUSE

Within the week, Elder Fleming called.

"I know your letter asked for privacy, but I thought I'd give you the opportunity to have a more intimate dialogue about your decision, away from the Kingdom Hall," he said.

I wondered if Michael had anything to do with him reaching out. I was a little flattered that Fleming cared but also knew there was no hope of him changing my mind. I was exhausted from the stress of this ordeal and wanted things to start settling down. Still, the fact that I hadn't felt heard in the previous meeting with the Elders made me consider this might be a good time to get my point of view addressed or at least acknowledged.

With some ambivalence, I said yes. We arranged for me to go to his house the following evening.

That night, when Michael phoned, I told him about the meeting.

He hesitated a bit too long before responding, which made me suspect he wasn't all that surprised.

"Well, D, I think this will be just what you need. He's smart and really understands the scriptures."

"That's true," I said cautiously.

"Make sure to bring all of your questions and take really good notes," he advised.

Fleming answered the door wearing shorts and a denim button-up shirt that was open halfway. I could see his chest hair. I didn't see his wife or any signs of her presence, except for the faint smell of cooked ground beef hanging in the air. He went in for a hug and I stiffened as the bare part of his chest touched the front of my shirt. I was sweating heavily, and my shirt was damp. He must have sensed my discomfort, because he said something about the awful heat.

He invited me inside and walked me down the hall.

"Let's go into my study," he said.

I followed him. "Is Patience here?"

"She's out on a Bible call," he said.

In the study, he directed me to a couch. He offered me a glass of water, then poured himself a hefty glass of Scotch, walked to the door, and closed it. His bookshelves were lined with rows of literature sold at the Kingdom Hall and stacks of old *Watchtower* and *Awake!* magazines.

He wheeled a desk chair toward me and sat. "Did you bring your questions?"

Something was different about him; he didn't seem like the same person I knew—or, rather, the Elder I knew. There was an unfamiliar intimacy in his manner and voice. His blue eyes focused on me so intensely, I felt suffocated. Wiping sweat from my upper lip, I diverted my eyes to the notebook on my lap and nodded.

"I understand that you still have some concerns and confusion about the interpretation of the literature when it comes to Jehovah's selection of Christians who'll receive salvation from Armageddon," he said.

This confirmed that he'd talked to Michael, because that was the issue we'd been endlessly discussing. I couldn't blame him. He was trying to save my soul, just like I'd once thought I was saving his.

I launched into my spiel. Using skills I'd learned in speech class to build my point, I felt articulate and confident.

When I finished, he leaned forward in his seat. "Darls, you've always been such an excellent example of a young woman in The Truth," he said. "It is natural to have doubts, especially when you're exposed to Satan and worldly temptations. University life can open you up to multiple dangers, as well as exposure to your disfellowshipped sister, who is steeped in the devil's playground."

Exposure, I thought. *What a strange choice of words to use for a family member.*

"She's chosen to fornicate with Satan's followers in a modern-day Sodom and Gomorrah. I understand why you'd feel discouraged." He said this with distaste, as if her lifestyle could contaminate him.

I didn't like that jab at my sister.

He rolled his chair a little closer.

"Does she still associate with *Playboy*?" he asked.

"She's at home," I answered, knowing this answer was vague but not so different from how he answered my questions—ducking and diving from the truth. The real truth, at least.

He took my lined notebook from my lap and read some of my questions silently to himself. He cleared his throat and took a long sip of his drink.

"Well, you see, Sister Darls," he said, his voice less animated than when he'd spoken about Susie. He pulled out a *Watchtower* magazine and read, "'The point is that Christians have implicit trust in their heavenly Father; they do not question what He tells them through His written word and organization.'"

"This argument that Jehovah is the ultimate authority and there is no questioning allowed no longer fits in with my sense of right and wrong," I said, feeling shaky. *Plus, this article was written by a Jehovah's Witness—just some man*, I thought. *It has no real Biblical authority.*

He pulled out another *Watchtower* magazine and read: "'There is a people who are different and everyone knows they are different and not part of the world. They are Jehovah's Witnesses.'"

That *Watchtower* magazine was dated 1968.

"You're either serving Jehovah or Satan—there is nothing in between," he said.

I realized that coming to this meeting had been a bad idea. *What exactly did I expect?* I berated myself.

Fleming continued, telling me to trust in Jehovah and that questioning his word indicated my failure of faith.

I felt insulted and resentful. I was angry at Jehovah's Witnesses for not being what I'd thought they were, angry I couldn't return to my former state of ignorance, and angry that I'd been duped for so long. But mostly I was angry that I had lost my entire social support system and that things would never be the same with Michael and La Toya.

"Look, I didn't try to lose my faith," I countered. "But how do I believe something that doesn't feel authentic or real any longer? Thank you for giving me this time, Brother Fleming, but I have to go now."

"Darls, it's important that you pray and ask for Jehovah to remove the shackles that are binding you to temptation."

This isn't about temptation, I thought, *it's about a belief system that is twisted*. I wanted to be on the other side of that closed study door. I stood up, opened the door, and began walking out to my car.

Fleming followed me. I didn't notice he'd removed his shirt until I opened my car door. He slung his arm on the roof and suddenly I was trapped in his armpit, facing him. I could smell his body odor—a combination of deodorant and the musk of his perspiration.

"Sometimes we all feel tempted to do things that are forbidden," he croaked.

He grabbed my hand.

"Darls, you're so sweet."

I felt my knees give a little and before I knew what was happening, he closed his eyes and moved in for a kiss, landing it on my lips.

I jerked my face away, pulled my hand from his grip, and leapt into the car. My legs were shaking so hard I could barely operate the pedals.

"Thank you for your help," I stammered as I drove off.

And he had helped me. He had just pushed me even farther from "The Truth."

I woke up the next morning wishing the night before had been a bad dream.

As I oriented myself, the word "hypocrite" came to mind. Fleming had accused me of being led into temptation, when in truth it was him. *He* was the sexual deviant. I was seeking answers, and *he* was after sex. I wanted to talk to Michael and La Toya, but how could they deal with this on top of me leaving? *What if they don't believe me?* I flashed back to the abusive experience with my dead uncle, and feelings of impurity flooded my entire body.

I needed a long, hot shower.

Susie came back that night after a whirlwind modeling trip to Japan. As she settled in the bedroom with her suitcase, I told her every detail of my meeting with Fleming.

Susie was horrified and called Tina and Phil in Florida. Although they were forbidden to speak with her, Susie told them it was an emergency, and they stayed on the line.

Without hesitation, Susie described the incident; then blurted, "I thought you should know," and hung up.

It didn't take me long to realize the consequences this would have, and I imagined the gossip working its way through the Kingdom Hall grapevine.

Tina called me a few hours later.

"Darls, I heard something happened between you and Elder Fleming—can you explain?"

Her voice was distant. She and Phil were good friends with Fleming and Patience.

"I went to a meeting with him at his house to discuss my questions," I said.

I didn't realize Phil was on the line too until he chimed in, "Why did you go to his house? Did you ask to spend time alone with him? Are you sure you were clear about *your* intentions? Fleming said you were wearing immodest clothing."

My heart raced. This meant he'd already talked with Fleming, who was clearly casting me as the inappropriate one in his story. I told them what I'd worn: baggy jeans, a polo shirt, and sneakers—not exactly the clothes of a seductress.

My mind was swirling, trying to catch up. Without thinking it through, I suggested that maybe the moment had been blown out of proportion. I didn't want any further Jehovah's Witness drama, and I knew I would be considered the culprit, the Jezebel, the liar. I was ill-equipped to deal with a controversy of this magnitude, much less take on the Governing Body of Jehovah's Witnesses. I was already afraid they would disfellowship me, and I just wanted to leave in peace.

Tina and Phil abruptly wrapped up the conversation. I was surprised that they were so easily suspicious of me, and I was deeply hurt by their betrayal.

I WAS A WATCHTOWER SLAVE

I didn't know what to do with my growing angst. The next day, still extremely unnerved, I drove to the local library and pulled *30 Years a Watchtower Slave* from the stacks. I sat down at a table and read the entire thing in one sitting.

The author referred to the religion as a totalitarian cult. I thought about that loaded label, *totalitarian*; I'd heard about the concept in history class repeatedly and wanted a specific definition. I went to the encyclopedia and looked it up: *An authoritarian government that does not allow for any opposition and has control over individual freedom, will, and thought.*

The author spoke of the Watchtower Society as a multimillion-dollar publishing company, with its primary goal being to sell literature. He'd left this "corrupt organization" after being a founding member and spending thirty years in the religion. He'd helped build an empire that included massive bank accounts and huge property holdings. He described Jehovah's Witnesses as a profit-seeking corporation that used propaganda to make millions off the followers who devoted their lives to it.

He provided inside secrets on the practice of indoctrination that begins when a person accepts their first *Watchtower* magazine. He broke down the specific steps used by the organization to manipulate and brainwash its followers. He also gave numerous examples of strategies used to get members to inform on other members, including relatives, to keep the religion free from anyone who represented a threat. I remembered how the Elders had tried to coerce me into turning in my own sister.

The organization he depicted was sinister and evil.

I was especially struck by this passage: *Before the uncanny victim realized it, he had surrendered all individualism, abandoned all personal thinking.*

My brain was in deprogramming mode. I could finally witness the depth and breadth of corruption perpetuated by the Worldwide Organization of the Watchtower Society, and it was truly appalling.

PART THREE
WHAT REMAINS

> My life had journeyed far beyond the precious era I'd shared with the Jacksons. As a teenager, I'd longed to be an adult... now, I wanted nothing more than to retreat into the safety of my adolescent friendship with Michael and La Toya.
>
> — Journal entry, September 4, 1977

> I just got home from a long day of work and school. My mind is still tangled and confused. In my English class today, we read a poem that struck me deeply—"The Love Song of J. Alfred Prufrock" by T.S. Eliot. It's about an old man struggling with whether to keep conforming to the expectations of society or live life on his own terms, knowing it would mean giving up everything familiar. That's me. If I give up the "Truth," I give up all the security and safety it has given me. I give up my dearest friends, La Toya and Michael. But I also know, deep inside, that I have no regrets about stepping away. I no longer believe the version of God they've given me. I've made up my mind. Now, I just have to live with the decision.
>
> — Journal entry, October 4, 1977

> Look at this, Darles, as if they are your own children, because they really are, you know.
>
> — Inscription from Michael, 1979

DISFELLOWSHIPPED

My former Bible student Cindy came into the restaurant where I worked one day and began asking my coworkers personal questions about me.

"Does Darls smoke?" she asked them. "Does she have a boyfriend? Does she take drugs?"

I knew the Elders must have sent her on a quest to covertly investigate me and bring back some dirt. *Why do they want to condemn my soul when I'm on my way out anyway?*

Infuriated, I called Cindy.

"I heard you were snooping around at my job, asking my coworkers and bosses questions about my behavior," I spat into the phone. "Why don't you ask me directly?"

"I don't owe you an explanation," she said. "And I can't speak with you because you're disfellowshipped."

"No, I'm not, that's impossible!"

"It was announced on Sunday by Elder Nathaniel," she said smugly, then repeated the statement Michael's brother-in-law had publicly shared, "*Darls Centola has been disfellowshipped for conduct unbecoming a Christian.*'

You're an apostate. So don't call me because I can't speak with you."

Then she hung up.

I couldn't believe it. *How could they make me look like an immoral person?* I'd been so careful.

I broke down in humiliation and rage and ran into my room. Collapsing onto my pillow, I baptized myself in a flood of tears. A reverse baptism, an undoing of this chapter of my life. I'd been so confident I knew Jehovah, and now I didn't even know how to pray to God.

I'd observed other Witnesses go through the torment of the disfellowshipping process, watched the public flogging of their reputation. *Darls Centola has been disfellowshipped for conduct unbecoming a Christian.*

I couldn't stop repeating it in my head—the accused sinner's name called out from the podium, the wording always the same. The implication was either fornication or sexually unacceptable behavior, and the punishment was banishment by all those in the religion. I hadn't done *anything* unbecoming of a Christian. Disfellowshipping was exactly what I'd tried to avoid when I wrote the letter and voluntarily left.

In retrospect, though, it all made perfect sense. Michael and La Toya had been calling me to question and debate my reasoning. When we spoke, I was armed with evidence about the false doctrine and mind-control aspects of the religion. Michael always listened to me intently and, by the end of our conversations, I sensed his own confusion. I imagined he and La Toya were seeking their own answers to the questions I'd been posing and had likely shared my opinions with their devout sister, Rebbie, and her husband, Nathaniel the Elder.

It was fitting that Brother Nathaniel had made the public announcement of my excommunication at the Kingdom Hall. It was his family, after all, that most needed protection from my wicked ways.

My questioning of the doctrine had most likely been deemed apostate, and I couldn't deny that I fit the description of the word: I was indeed a person who renounced a religious or political belief or principle. But the connotation of apostate was so charged. I looked it up in the dictionary and discovered synonyms like dissenter, heretic, nonconformist, defector, deserter, traitor, turncoat, and renegade. I liked the idea of being a renegade—but *heretic* seemed medieval and brought up visions of the Spanish Inquisition, where people were tortured and killed for not being Christians. Shunning was essentially a modern-day form of psychological torture.

I'd never known anyone disfellowshipped under the terms of being an apostate, though I'd seen plenty of teen and adult Jehovah's Witnesses leave of their own accord.

I had been ostracized for voicing dissent, and for leaving the religion voluntarily. The process of disfellowshipping always included a formal meeting with the individual to discuss their transgressions and provide them with an opportunity to repent—but in my situation, there was nothing for me to repent. Fleming had undoubtedly twisted and skewed the story of our meeting to accuse me of sexual transgression. I was now considered "dangerous"—yet *he* was the predator. *He* was the one who should repent.

I was curious if there had been an exchange between the Elders in my congregation and the Watchtower Society in New York. It appeared they'd made a collaborative decision to disfellowship me for electing to leave. I thought back to the meeting with the Elders at the Kingdom Hall—how they were more concerned with my interactions with Michael than my questions. It was also obvious that Michael was getting guidance to refute my skepticism. I thought further back, to when Brother Long asked me to tell Michael to cut his hair. My mentoring Michael had been on the Elder's radar since we'd begun studying together.

My sin was being a nonbeliever, but being Michael's friend led to my downfall.

SOLO FLIGHT

I never heard from Tina and Phil again—or the Rolands, for that matter. But what did I expect? That was the process of excommunication: a complete cut-off.

My heart ached with longing for Michael and La Toya.

It was such an empty feeling to be on this side of disfellowshipping. I couldn't just pick up the phone and call my friends. *They see me as misguided and under the influence of the Devil*, I reminded myself every time I was tempted to do so. I felt that way about other people who had left The Truth.

I wondered who would become Michael's future Bible teacher and worried about his shyness with someone new. I imagined he felt as if I'd failed him. The guilt I was feeling directly conflicted with the strength of my new convictions. My head was so busy trying to resolve things that at times I found myself talking out loud to imagined listeners like the Elders, Michael, La Toya, Katherine, Tina, and Cindy. I was repeatedly explaining myself, attempting to be heard. How ironic that I was speaking to no one; it was essentially the same as when I spoke with the Elders;

no one heard or received my words then, and no one was doing so now.

I had no one to talk to but phantoms. Susie was so busy, and when she was around, she couldn't be less interested in Jehovah's Witnesses. She moved on, and her life was full of first love excitement and a busy modeling career.

I missed Michael; my heart hurt. I was experiencing so much loss, and while the process was painful, I was also growing and evolving in new ways.

I threw myself into my education in a whole new way after leaving my religion. The future immediately became something I could allow myself to invest in. Although this new future was filled with uncertainty, it was better than a false one. It was scary to emerge into the world, but my compass was shifting.

I started planning a trip to Europe the following summer and bought the book *Frommer's Europe on 10 Dollars a Day*. While reading it one day in an English Literature class, a girl named Nancy sat next to me.

"Who are you going to Europe with?" she inquired.

I'd seen her before. She was outgoing and seemed to be popular, unlike me.

"Just me, so far," I said. "I plan to get a Eurail ticket and a youth hostel pass. People do it all the time, and this book helps with all kinds of useful information."

"Can I go with you?" she asked.

I was surprised by her assertiveness. "Sure," I said.

And just like that, Nancy joined me in planning what was now *our* backpacking trip.

My new life expanded quickly, but it was filled with growing pains.

I was adrift in this unfamiliar world searching for a new sense of identity and a redefined truth. Embracing my authentic self and breaking free from blind obedience became essential to my journey. Although I wanted a sense of belonging, I had some principles that were unwavering. It was important to maintain my morals. Nancy and her friend Jane were now including me in their activities, and we were swiftly becoming close, but they were miles ahead of me socially: they were going out to clubs and having sex. I couldn't imagine myself behaving that way. I discreetly excused myself from many activities that felt uncomfortable.

I still suffered from a deep loneliness.

My lack of confidence and experience was a huge barrier. I had so much catching up to do. I had no idea how to engage with boys, even though I was consumed by the thought of them. Now that I was allowed to be a regular teen, I had no skills at it. Plus, my heart still belonged to Michael. I missed the ease and comfort of our connection profoundly. I didn't believe I'd ever find that level of emotional closeness again. He knew me completely.

CLANDESTINE REUNIONS

One night, about a month after getting excommunicated, I had a dream I was standing naked in front of the congregation.

Michael was sitting in the front row, covering his eyes with his hands and saying, "No, no, this is all a misunderstanding."

His brother-in-law Nathaniel stood over him wagging a foot-long finger and pointing at me. Later in that same dream, Michael was calling me, but I couldn't get to the phone.

I woke up disoriented, and for a moment believed I'd made a mistake by leaving the religion. That tormenting feeling of having to choose came rushing back. Then, awakening more fully, I realized the phone was ringing in the other room.

It must have rung fifteen times before I could answer. It was La Toya.

"Darls, Mother and I have been talking. Michael and I have been so down since you left. Mother thinks it's okay for us to get together occasionally. In fact, she insists. We just need to be discreet. Michael agrees."

I couldn't believe my ears. Was I still dreaming? Why would Katherine approve? She was such a devout Jehovah's Witness. It had been a couple months since I'd spoken with any of the Jacksons. I was thrilled to hear they were missing me as much as I missed them. I suspected Katherine's approval meant she hoped I might find my way back into the fold; I was okay with that if it meant I could have my friends back.

There was one caveat: The terms of our reunion mandated that we keep our forbidden friendship a secret. I couldn't go to their house if there was any chance Rebbie or Nathaniel—or any other Jehovah's Witnesses—were near.

I was elated. I didn't love the fact that I was now a dirty little secret, but it was better than having no contact.

La Toya and I planned to meet at Casa Vega that very night, the perfect place for a clandestine meeting.

The hostess greeted me as I walked in the door.

"I'm meeting a friend," I said. I'm sure she'd heard that line more than once in this dark hideaway restaurant. "Oh, I see her!"

La Toya was blotting the excess oil off her tortilla chip with a cocktail napkin. She was wearing a red cloth hat and a red tight-ribbed sweater that matched the Naugahyde leather of the booth. She was startled when I approached, jumped up, and gave me a big hug.

"I'm so happy to see you!" she said. "This whole time has been so hard. We miss you."

I was relieved to hear those words. "I miss you too," I said, sliding into the booth.

"Have you considered coming back to the Kingdom Hall?" she asked.

"No, I'm not planning to come back," I said honestly. "I don't know if I ever could."

We quickly changed the subject. It was so easy to revert to our natural rhythm together and we spent a few hours catching up.

Michael called me that night and I was so happy to hear his voice. We easily returned to our normal selves; for the most part, we simply avoided the subject of church. When it was broached, I was careful with how I presented my beliefs—or, rather, lack of them. I knew that my firm arguments opposing the Church's doctrines were what had caused me to be disfellowshipped in the first place.

"Darls, I don't get it," Michael said at one point. "How could you give up the prospect of eternal life? Especially when the end is so near?"

"Michael, how could I possibly feel okay about living forever in a world that excludes my family?" I retorted.

In response he quoted Christ's words in Matthew 10:34, suggesting that Witnesses should expect their beliefs to cause family divisions.

"I know, Michael, but I can't imagine being happy with everlasting life if I know my loved ones have been struck dead in Armageddon," I said. "Maybe I'd rather die with them."

Michael was quiet for a bit—and then responded exactly as I'd expected.

"Jehovah knows all," he said softly. "He knows your heart and He will protect you. If you can trust in God, you don't need to worry about how you will feel. Let Him hold you in his loving arms."

It was fascinating to hear him use the same logic I'd taught him, the exact phrases I had used to console him when he'd fretted about these same issues. Fascinating, and sad.

I tried a new tactic.

"Okay, Michael. We are taught the end of the world will not occur until every person on earth has a chance to hear and accept or reject Jehovah's way of life—but what about a child, let's say an impoverished child in Mexico or a Buddhist child in China? How can they be responsible for making such choices? It just seems outlandish."

Again, Michael quoted scripture and spouted canned responses. Then he was silent for a few beats, and I could tell he was getting equally frustrated. Finally, he changed the subject.

"I went to the skating rink last night with La Toya and Kathy and Kim Richards," he said.

This time, *I* went quiet. I was totally crushed. I felt left out, and maybe a little jealous.

Before I responded, he said in a rush, "I'm so sorry, D; so, so sorry. I knew that would hurt your feelings. And we did try to call you last night, but I admit it was last-minute."

"D, if you'd come back to the Kingdom Hall, we wouldn't have all these problems," Michael said, almost pleading. "We could go back to how it was before."

But even if that was what I wanted, it wasn't that simple. I'd have to repent. I'd also be separated, expected to sit in the back of the Kingdom Hall, leave before the end of the meeting, and speak to no one. That was the process required to be considered worthy of reinstatement, and there were no time frames or guarantees. It was solely up to the discretion of the governing body of Elders. I thought about the Elders. I imagined them actively campaigning to keep me away from the Jacksons.

I didn't want to stay on the phone any longer. I was filled once again with humiliation and grief, but also a new feeling—relief that I'd managed to escape this cruel religion.

I told Michael I had to pick up my brother from karate and we hung up.

I cried until I fell back to sleep.

The next morning, La Toya called and brought up the roller-skating incident. Michael must have shared my disappointment with her.

I got the sense they wanted forgiveness for leaving me out. I understood their difficult position, but that didn't mean I was any less hurt.

She quoted a *Watchtower* magazine, unsurprisingly, about praying for a change of heart.

She was thinking about me, when meanwhile all I wanted was the same for her and Michael.

CHAINS FALLING OFF

I felt compelled to write La Toya a seven-page letter, explaining my point of view.

My inner instincts are to love my family above all else, I wrote. The love that I have for God is phenomenal and I have utter appreciation for Him, but my love for my family and God are not comparable. I can't leave one for the other. It's like someone asking me, if your mother or father were drowning, who would you save? Of course, the question is unanswerable. I would choose both because I couldn't think of giving up either. Well, that's what the Jehovah's Witness organization is asking me to do—to choose between my parents, who don't accept the teachings of Jehovah God and his true Organization.

I sent the letter, but she said she never got it.

La Toya and I had a new favorite spot on Hollywood Boulevard, where we'd park and observe the colorful parade of characters passing by. It was like watching a movie, and our conversation revolved around who and what we saw—a new normal that allowed us to converse comfortably.

Not all talk of religion could be avoided, however.

"Darls, Michael and I want you to read this article," she would often say, then hand me Jehovah's Witness literature with marked passages.

She and Michael were becoming more steadfast in their faith as a result of me losing mine. Had it still mattered to me, I would have been impressed with their progress. But now it all felt upside down to me.

As a seventeen-year-old, I was adjusting to my new life of freedom. I slowly allowed myself to loosen up, saying yes to the occasional party invitation and letting myself enjoy being a bit boy crazy. Though I was getting closer to Nancy and Jane and a few other classmates my age, none of those friendships held the safety of my old relationships with La Toya and Michael. It seemed like nothing could ever replace that closeness. Knowing those times were over filled me with a constant ache.

I consumed myself with researching and organizing my summer trip to Europe. My plan was to travel via trains with a backpack for two months, beginning in June of 1977. Jane joined too and we became a busy trio—planning, buying gear, studying maps, selecting destinations, and developing itineraries.

I liked having friends my age, but we were still miles apart developmentally. While La Toya and Michael felt so much more innocent than me, these new friends made me seem like the naïve one.

FLYING THE COOP

In June of 1977, I left for Amsterdam.

It was hard to believe my parents had been so against me being a Jehovah's Witness but had no objections to me flying alone to Amsterdam at seventeen. I was so inexperienced in the world; I approached going to a foreign country alone as if I were going to Disneyland, expecting signposts all along the way. I believed my travel book, youth hostel membership, Eurail pass, and backpack were all I needed to navigate the unknown.

Still, I was on fire and in love with the foreign sights, new cultures, languages, architecture, and international characters. It was exactly what I wanted—freedom to quench my thirst for expansion through *lived* experiences. I was able to use my French here and there, and discovered I was good at reading maps and train tables.

Fireworks lit up the sky on my eighteenth birthday. I was camping on the beach in the French Riviera with Nancy, Jane, and three Swedish backpackers we had met in Paris. One of them was a handsome, athletic guy named Anders;

we liked each other. Even though I was no longer bound by my old religious beliefs, I still felt loyalty to Michael. There was a part of me that felt guilty. But I couldn't deny how exciting it was to like a boy and be allowed to have my feelings. I imagined that the colorful display was for me, representing my personal Independence Day. It was the first time I had celebrated my birthday since I'd turned thirteen.

Anders and I became close, and we traveled together in this group of six for several weeks, from France to Italy to Switzerland. By the time we said goodbye in Geneva, we were plotting ways he could move to the US so we could be together. This felt like the tipping point that allowed me to heal the pain of my separation and alienation from Michael, who for so long had lived in my heart as my true love. My feelings for Anders didn't feel forbidden. I was free to open myself to their delights and enjoy my state of limerence. Anders was real; the only obstacle between us was an ocean. The barriers between Michael and I were much larger.

I came home from Europe floating on a cloud of newfound love and looked forward to Anders calling me every few days from Sweden.

A month after I returned home from Europe, Anders proposed that we get married—it would allow him to get a green card and work legally in the US. He was only nineteen and I was only eighteen, but I'd been desensitized to teens getting married—it happened all the time for

Jehovah's Witnesses—so it didn't seem like a crazy idea to me.

While I'd been traveling, my parents had reunited and moved from Mom's dinky apartment to a rented house. I was surprised to discover that they didn't have a bedroom for me.

"You said a hundred times that you were moving out when you turned eighteen," my mother said.

I couldn't disagree, but felt I'd been overlooked once again.

Luckily, I was on my own high, with an adult trajectory that included Anders's impending arrival. I put all my belongings in a huge wardrobe box, which I stored in a closet, and for the next few months lived out of my backpack and slept on my parents' living room floor. In the meantime, I got myself back into school and enjoyed fantasies of reuniting with my new Swedish fiancé.

First, I had to find us a place to live; Anders and I decided to get an apartment together. We were both working to save money toward the first and last month's rent. I'd never thought I'd live with someone before marriage, but this was turning into a year of firsts.

THE WIZ

When I returned from Europe, Michael and La Toya were in New York, where Michael was filming *The Wiz*. One afternoon, I received a call from them. Far from home and the eyes of the Kingdom Hall, they invited me to come visit them for an extended stay.

Together, they filled me in with the details of their big city adventures and asked about my own experiences in recent months.

"How was backpacking in Europe?" La Toya asked.

"Yeah, D, how was your first time leaving the country?" Michael chimed in.

It was so good to hear their voices. I'd forgotten how easy it was to laugh with them.

I shared a few stories but held back on the part about meeting Anders—I didn't know how it would be received. A familiar rush of shame, the kind I associated with being disfellowshipped, came over me. The telephone call had triggered something raw and tender. I listened as they recounted the fun they were having in New York, interrupting each other and squealing with excitement.

La Toya, I knew, would be thrilled to hear about Anders, but Michael would be crushed. Michael and I had a life plan, however fantastical it was. We had made so many mutual promises to better the lives of children together. Although my being disfellowshipped had put a huge wedge between us, my getting married would create an insurmountable gap.

I could feel Michael's enthusiasm as he told me about his new friend Dick Gregory, a comedian and activist.

"Darls, there are so many ways we can become involved and fight against hatred and inequality," he said. "Dick is a believer and promoter of nonviolent civil rights. He's been arrested tons of times and he's a feminist, fighting for women's freedom, even though he's a man. Isn't that interesting?"

I honestly believed if Michael had not been born into show business, his calling would have been as a social justice advocate—he cared so deeply about the woes of the world.

Toward the end of the conversation, they told me more about the film. La Toya said the days on set were long and that if I came for a visit, we could explore New York together and then meet up with Michael after filming. They asked me to come at least half a dozen times, culminating in an offer to mail me an airline ticket the next day.

"Just come!" La Toya urged.

I was longing to go, but realized it necessitated me finally sharing my big news.

"You guys won't believe this, but I'm getting married," I said.

La Toya gasped with delight—and then I heard a click. Michael had hung up.

OH, GOD

The next time the Jacksons were back in Los Angeles, La Toya told me about Michael's disappointment on hearing I was getting married. It dampened my euphoria, as I receded to the place in my heart that loved Michael—the same place that felt as though he could never love me back.

Michael, La Toya, and I saw each other a few times after they returned. In November of 1977, two nights before I got married, we went to the movies to see *Oh, God!*.

I was living in a small one-bedroom apartment with Anders by this point. La Toya came to my apartment alone, with the plan being to fetch Michael on the way to the movies. I introduced her to Anders, who was sitting on a recliner. He stood up, towering over her, and they said hello. I felt proud of my little apartment and hoped La Toya would approve of Anders.

She giggled shyly as they shook hands. "Good to meet you," she said. Her cheeks twitched with a nervous smile.

We hurried out and as we descended the stairs she said, "He's really handsome, Darls! By the way, Michael doesn't know I came here first—or that you live with your fiancé."

Once again, I had a flashback of being disfellowshipped and that familiar feeling of being unclean came up, fast and furious. It was as if I'd committed a transgression of some kind by living with a man, even though I knew it wasn't. I hated that this power still loomed over me, since it was based on a moral code I no longer subscribed to.

It was interesting that La Toya could tolerate my sin, but Michael couldn't. I know my choices were hurtful. From their perspective, they had lost me to Satan.

When we picked up Michael, he was polite but distant. He made little eye contact, and his body language was guarded and stiff. He waved at me but offered no hug. He got in the back seat and asked La Toya to turn up a song on the radio he really liked. Later, La Toya told me he had cried a few times earlier that day when he'd talked about me. That broke my heart. As much as I was excited about my new life, letting go of my old one was far more difficult than I'd imagined.

In the theater, Michael and I sat next to each other. Our arms touched—our old, puppy-like way of expressing affection—and a part of me wished we could travel back to that time. We laughed hard during the movie and exchanged a few glances during the funny parts. At one point when Michael touched my arm, he held my gaze for a few beats, and I could see both laughter and sadness in his eyes.

The film had broken the ice and it felt good to be together again. For the rest of the movie, we exchanged frequent glances during the funny moments; our connection was still there. *What a relief*, I thought. Michael's eyes had revealed his heart, and it was wide open, even if only for a few shared laughs in a dark movie theater.

After the movie, La Toya dropped Michael off first, then drove me home.

"My mom and I will see you at the wedding!" she announced before driving off.

The morning of my wedding, La Toya called to say they couldn't make it. I was devastated, but it was fitting. This pivotal moment called me to move forward in my life—to look ahead—and as much as it hurt, the Jacksons were becoming part of my past. They spoke the language of Jehovah's Witnesses, which was exclusionary. I was one of the outsiders now, and the chasm between us was too wide to bridge.

Over the next year, La Toya and I still got together occasionally. Instead of hanging out in my little toy of a car, however, she would pick me up in her mother's red Mercedes. We'd go to our usual spot on Hollywood Boulevard or by Westlake near downtown LA.

La Toya liked to talk about her family; I think she needed a place to vent. I was a safe space for her, and I enjoyed being her confidante.

Michael did not attend our occasional reunions. He was busy recording as a solo artist. His first album outside of

Motown, *Off the Wall*, had just been released, and it had four hit songs in the top 10 of the *Billboard* Hot 100. La Toya was so happy for her brother and often shared how much she missed him because he was traveling so much.

    She also told me that Michael choked up during the recording of the song "She's Out of My Life" because he was thinking of me and the loss of our friendship.

    I wouldn't allow myself to believe that. He was all over the pages of gossip magazines these days, dating Tatum O'Neal and bringing model Brooke Shields to award shows. I thought for sure he had forgotten me—but La Toya said that was all for public display.

CHILDREN OF MANY LANDS

In August 1979, two years after I got married, I was working in the office at Cal Prep, helping Mrs. Yardum prepare for the fall semester. I felt a strong obligation to her for putting me and my sister through high school on scholarship. It was a debt that could never be repaid in full.

On that day, Mrs. Yardum announced we were to work straight from nine to noon with no distractions. This meant no side conversations and no lingering phone calls.

"Focus, focus, focus," she said in her high-pitched, fading southern accent—even though she was the one most likely to get sidetracked telling stories. The start of a new school year was approaching, and enrollment at Cal Prep continued to grow. My job was to review transcripts and tabulate credits for the juniors and seniors, which was something I'd done with Mrs. Yardum for years. I worked quickly and efficiently, and most importantly, I could anticipate her needs.

I hadn't talked to Michael since we'd seen *Oh, God!*; these days, I was connected to him only through La Toya.

His skyrocketing popularity and me being married and disfellowshipped was the final straw.

The office phone rang; I reached for it.

"Cal Prep, how may I help you?" I asked.

"Is Darls working today?" The voice was muffled and sounded artificially deep.

"This is Darls," I answered.

The caller said thank you and hung up, leaving me perplexed. Mrs. Yardum gave me a sideways glance that meant *get back to work.*

Fifteen minutes or so later, a man arrived with a package for me. I heard my name and turned to see him handing a gift-wrapped bundle to the principal, Andre.

"Secret admirer?" He handed me the package with a sly smile.

I shrugged and started to unwrap it, Andre and Mrs. Yardum peeking over my shoulder as I did.

Right away, I noticed Michael's large, scrawling signature on the gold and white wrapping paper. His handwriting was unmistakable. There was no card, just a note Michael had written on the paper in blue ink:

Thank you for being my friend through the years. Love, M.J.

I put it together: the phone call had been Michael, using a disguised voice, and the man was Michael's driver. I grabbed the package and ran outside in the hopes of catching Michael in the car.

The black Rolls-Royce was already pulling into traffic on Ventura Boulevard. I could barely make out the outline of Michael's head through the tinted back window. His hair was cut short. I stood there with the gift in my hands, waiting to see if he would turn around to look, but he didn't.

Back in the office, I unwrapped the package to find a hardbound coffee table book. It was a collection of black-and-white photographs of children from around the world, entitled *Children of Many Lands*. Michael's inscription read: *Look at this Darls as if they are your own children, because they really are you know. Love Michael Jackson 79.*

Later that afternoon, the office phone rang, and I answered.

"Hi, D, it's me, Michael. Did you get a chance to unwrap the gift?" He started giggling.

"Oh, Michael, I ran outside to try and catch you, but you were already driving away," I said. "Thank you so much for the book—it's beautiful."

"I have a copy of it too, and I've been wanting to get you one for a long time, only it's out of print," he said. "I had to hunt it down by going to a bunch of used bookstores. I was so happy when I found it." He paused. "Are you going to get in trouble for being on the phone at work?"

I looked up and saw my bosses staring at me.

"Mrs. Yardum and Andre are sending you a big hello."

He laughed. "Enjoy the book, D. Let it sink in and remember what we always talked about. Let me know how you like it."

I'd forgotten how much I loved when he called me "D." I wanted to hang on to this moment as long as I could. I laughed, which he then imitated, as he always did.

There was so much I wanted to say and so much I wanted to ask, but Michael said he was rushing off to the studio. He suggested we go to the movies when he finished in a few weeks, and then we hung up.

I went back to reviewing transcripts, but my mind was no longer on my work. I was thinking about Michael and missing him.

Missing us and the irreplaceable connection we had.

THE FAREWELL

Five years later, Anders told me La Toya called and left a message, along with a new phone number.

It was 1983. I was twenty-three years old, separated from my husband. I hadn't heard from La Toya or Michael in years, so this was a welcome surprise. My life felt like a mess; I was desperate for the comfort of an old friend, a trusted shoulder to lean on.

I nervously dialed. La Toya answered. Within minutes, we chatted like no time had passed.

"It's good to hear your voice, Darls," she said. "Can you come over? We remodeled the whole house. You won't recognize it—we even have a movie theater. Are you busy right now?"

I grabbed my keys and drove to the Jacksons' Encino estate. The guard at the gate called the house and then pressed the button to open the massive iron gates. As I drove down the long, winding driveway, I saw a new mansion where the old family home had stood. I parked among a familiar lineup of Mercedes and Rolls-Royces and was greeted by a crew of barking Doberman Pinschers. One of them I recognized—Hitler, a vicious dog I had met before. I stayed frozen in my car, afraid to get out.

A housekeeper appeared, shouting at the dogs in Spanish, then led me to the kitchen.

"Miss Jackson is upstairs," she said. "She will be down. Please sit."

I slid into the red leather booth built into the kitchen. Everything around me gleamed, staged and perfect, like a model home. It didn't feel lived in; it felt empty.

As I sat there, I kept glancing at the small TV mounted on the wall, half-watching the news. Every so often, I felt like I was being watched—specifically by Michael. I thought I heard his familiar giggle, caught a flicker of movement at the edge of my vision, like a shadow slipping out of sight. It felt like I was inside a fairy tale, where the prince remained invisible, appearing only when no one was looking.

Finally, Katherine Jackson walked in and greeted me with her warm, familiar hug.

"I've missed you, Darls! How are you doing? Are you working?"

"Yes, Mrs. Jackson. I'm teaching now at Cal Prep—history, drama, and psychology."

We talked until La Toya appeared a few minutes later. She hugged me tightly, then led me upstairs to her new suite. The room was unrecognizable—white plush carpet, a gold-trimmed fireplace, satin chairs, and an elegant sitting area. It was a far cry from the tiny bedroom she'd once shared with Janet.

We settled into overstuffed white chairs and talked for hours, catching up on old friends, the Kingdom Hall, our families. La Toya kept interrupting to mention how happy Michael had been to hear I was visiting, repeatedly buzzing him on the intercom.

"Michael, where are you? Darls is here."

He didn't answer.

She told me he'd been studying the Bible with Fleming since I was disfellowshipped—and that they'd grown close.

My heart sank. I never told either of them what had happened between me and Fleming.

She went back to the intercom.

"Really, don't bother," I said. "If Michael is close to Fleming, he won't want to see me."

"You're crazy," she replied. "We've missed you so much. Michael, Mother, and I always talk about you. Let me try once more."

This time, he picked up.

"Michael, Darls is here. Where are you?"

I heard his voice over the receiver.

"I can't come in to say hi, but tell her I saw her in the kitchen."

A lump rose in my throat. I knew it—he had been watching me.

"Tell her she's beautiful," he added quietly. "Tell her I love her."

La Toya's voice softened, confused. "What is going on with you, Michael?"

It felt like something broke inside me.

Still, I kept smiling, talking, refusing to fall apart. La Toya and I chatted about boys, sex, clothes, the people we knew, and the faith we'd once shared. She confessed that she still believed but didn't attend meetings anymore—that after I left, something shifted in her. She asked if there was any chance I'd come back, that maybe I could even work for the family so we could all be together again.

"No, La Toya," I said. "That's impossible. As far as I'm concerned, Jehovah's Witnesses is a cult."

She looked away, shifting in her chair. I regretted how bluntly I spoke—it wasn't what I meant to say—but the mention of Fleming left me raw.

We moved on, and the awkwardness faded.

That afternoon, I mourned the loss of my childhood. As a teenager, I longed to grow up, to leave it all behind. And now, all I wanted was to crawl back into the safety of that time, to be young again, with Michael and La Toya.

We tried to stay in touch after that meeting. There were occasional phone calls, but eventually her number changed, and our lives moved forward.

Years later, while revisiting my journals, I finally admitted something I had always known but never dared to say out loud:

Michael Jackson was my first love.

It wasn't infatuation, and it wasn't just friendship. It was the meeting of two souls who saw and understood each other with a clarity that felt like it belonged to another world.

I traveled the earth, fell in and out of love, but nothing ever touched the magic of what we shared. There was a purity in him, a kind of goodness so fragile the world could never protect it.

We were held back by invisible walls—our fears, his father, the weight of our religion, the pressure of his fame. I used to wonder what might have happened if we had given ourselves permission to love without fear. If he had left when I did. If I had waited.

But there are no answers to questions like that.

And so, in the quiet of that realization, I let my heart break completely—knowing that only in its breaking could I finally begin to heal.

EPILOGUE

The year I resigned as a Jehovah's Witness was the same year Michael Jackson went into the studio to create *Off the Wall*—an album that would become a global phenomenon. Its innovative sound and emotionally intelligent lyrics catapulted it to one of the best-selling albums of all time. Producer Quincy Jones recalled that Michael wept during every take of "She's Out of My Life."

I've come to believe that, in part, his grief may have stemmed from the loss of our friendship. In his memoir *Moonwalk*, he described that year as the loneliest of his life—a loneliness that fueled his creativity. "There was one girl who was a good friend to me. I liked her, but I was too embarrassed to tell her."

Michael's influence shaped the trajectory of my life. I became a sign language interpreter, earned a degree in social work, and spent years working with youth in foster care. Today, I am a Licensed Clinical Social Worker specializing in trauma recovery—including religious trauma—and certified in EMDR. From a clinical perspective, I can now see how both Michael and I endured layers of trauma, within our families and under the grip of a high-control religious group. After I was shunned, I experienced symptoms akin to PTSD.

In 1987, ten years after my resignation, Michael formally withdrew from the Church. The Jehovah's Witnesses' headquarters issued a press release stating they "no longer consider Michael Jackson to be one of Jehovah's Witnesses."

That same year, at twenty-eight, Michael left his family home—and his mother, a devout Witness. With the vision and resources to build the idyllic world promised by his former faith, he created Neverland.

Combining the eternal childhood of Peter Pan with his love for Disneyland, he created a sanctuary where thousands of underprivileged and ill children could indulge in endless play. Perhaps this was his way of healing himself. I believe his deep connection with children also reflected a distrust of adult authority figures—his father, the Elders of the Church, and possibly older figures in the music industry.

I believe both Michael and I suffered from Religious Trauma Syndrome—a condition experienced by those who leave rigid, high-control faiths. The psychological toll of deprogramming from an Orwellian belief system rooted in fear, purity culture, and divine punishment is profound. Reclaiming one's identity and autonomy takes time.

The Elder who exploited my vulnerability—and who also mentored Michael—was eventually expelled from the religion for sexual misconduct. Similar abuses by Jehovah's Witness Elders have been reported nationwide.

High-control groups often silence victims and prioritize institutional loyalty over individual well-being.

I usually avoid speaking publicly about the controversy surrounding Michael. Yet I'm often asked about his innocence. Despite a decade of FBI investigations, he was consistently exonerated of all charges.

Perhaps he was guilty only of being too naïve, innocent—and a victim of trial by the media. It's possible that the weight of those allegations broke him long before that fatal dose of anesthesia.

Michael was a known advocate for children. Recently, Australian music attorney Paul Dwyer created *Humanitarian*, a book and documentary chronicling Michael's visits to orphanages and hospitals worldwide. It documents a body of humanitarian work largely ignored by the media. Michael donated over $500 million to charity and remains the most philanthropic pop star in history, according to *Guinness World Records*. He was nominated twice for the Nobel Peace Prize, in 1998 and 2003. To this day, his estate donates 20 percent of its earnings to charity.

I hope my story helps illuminate Michael's humanity and rebalances the narrative around this extraordinary, often misunderstood figure.

I know others who've left the Jehovah's Witnesses have felt the same exile, grief, and loss of identity I experienced. If my younger self could read this now, I would tell her she was never unworthy, unlovable, or beyond saving.

To anyone who has experienced religious trauma: healing is possible. Seek support from those who understand—through therapy, support groups, or trusted allies. Rebuilding your identity outside a high-control faith is not only possible, it's empowering. The fear and shame instilled in you do not define you. Reclaiming your voice is your birthright.

Michael's music finds me when I least expect it. When it does, I remember—not just the boy I knew, but something pure and sacred in him, as we both searched for God and truth.

PART FOUR
PHOTO ALBUM

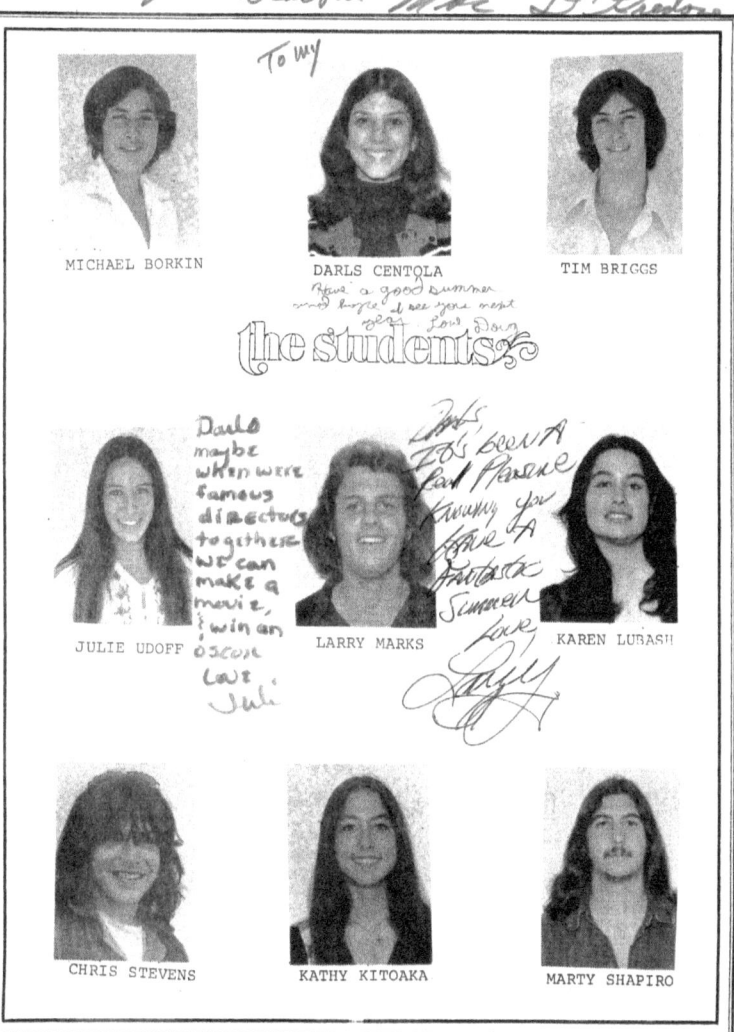

1974 yearbook photo of Darls Centola

1975 yearbook photos of Chris Brando (Marlon Brando's son) and Danny Bonaduce (child actor, The Partridge Family)

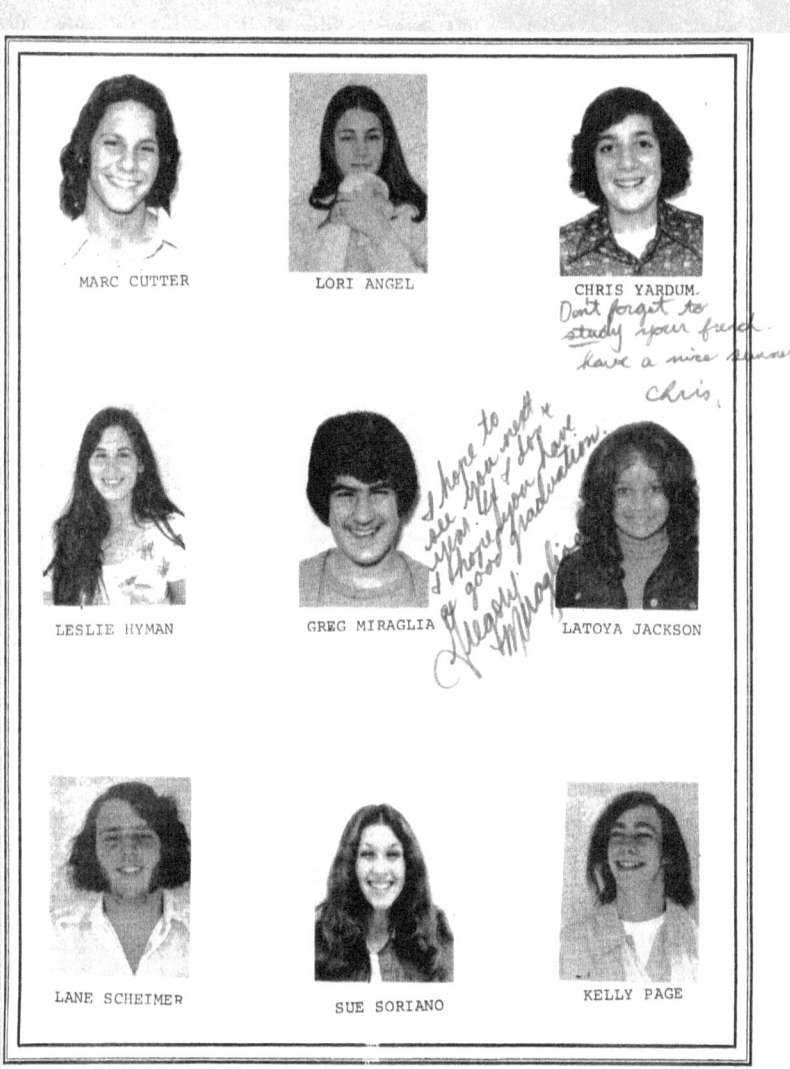

1974 yearbook photo of La Toya Jackson

1975 yearbook photo of Michael Jackson

1974 yearbook photos of Randy Jackson,
Kathy Richards, and Michael Jackson

WHO'S WHO

THIS YEAR'S CAL PREP STUDENTS HAVE CAST THE FOLLOWING VOTES:

CHARACTERISTICS	GALS	GUYS
MOST STUDIOUS	LORI ROWAN	LENNY REDER
MOST LIKELY TO SUCCEED	SUSIE CENTOLA	MICHAEL JACKSON
MOST OUTGOING	ROBIN COLMAN	LARRY MARKS
MOST ROWDY	DEBBIE LEBOWITZ	RYAN WATT
GREATEST CON ARTIST	KATHY RICHARDS	MIKE BORKIN
MOST SARCASTIC	LAURIE NEWMAN	ANDY BOSTON
MOST ARTISTIC	WENDY WARREN	MICHAEL JACKSON
MOST FEMININE AND MASCULINE	LA TOYA JACKSON	LARRY MARKS
MOST CONSERVATIVE	LORI ROWAN	CHRIS YARDUM
MOST LIBERAL	JULIE UDOFF	MARC CUTTER
NICEST DISPOSITION	ROZZIE GLANTZ	KELLY PAGE
BEST ACTOR AND ACTRESS	PATTY LEAVITT	RICHARD BREEN
BEST SENSE OF HUMOR	LORI ANGEL	MATHEW WARREN
BIGGEST SMILE	CINDY ALLEN / KIM ZAX	MARLON JACKSON
SEXIEST	MICHELLE MASCIOTRA	CHUCK HUENERGARDT
LONGEST LASTING LOVE AFFAIR	LESLIE HYMAN	CLAY CHAVANETTE
MOST RELIABLE	DARLS CENTOLA	JOHN YARDUM
SPARKLIEST EYES	SUE BARCLAY	JOHN MAHER
GROOVIEST	KATHY RICHARDS	CHUCK KATZ

Who's Who list, 1974 yearbook
Notable entries include Most Artistic: Michael Jackson and Lenny Reeder; and Best Dressed: Marlon Jackson and La Toya Jackson

LAURIE NEWMAN

I plan to enjoy my life. (single). Then continue my education in February, and look at all the beautiful guys.

I, LAURIE NEWMAN, Will my David Bowie tickets, with seat belts on the seats
    To Stephanie Norswing
A copy of "How To Relieve Your Tensions and Anxieties", and a bottle of Valium
    To Jan Tievsky
A Utopia school, where all the kids drive 1949 Volkswagens
    To Dave Danielsen
Five hundred bottles of nail polish
    To Michelle Masciotra
A deck of trick cards to beat Debbie at poker
    To Rozzie Glantz

STUART CANE

I plan to attend a state college, but I have not decided on which one at this point.

SUE CENTOLA

My plans are to study nutrition and to continue in dance. I shall possibly pursue an academic education next year.

I, SUE CENTOLA, Will

To Keith "Bilbo and His Mountain".

To Mike, the temperature at the top of the mountain.

To Wendy Watt, those "gay deceivers".

To Mrs. Yardum, all my love.

Sue Centola's senior will, 1974 yearbook

CAL PREP SCHOOL

1975 yearbook cover

GRADUATING CLASS OF '75

I'm going to make the best of my summer vacation, then major in Special Education at Northridge.

I, DARLS CENTOLA, Will to the following:

To La Toya: A rust colored Mercedes convertable
To Michael Jackson: A farm in the middle of the forest with animals, especially singing birds, sheep and Llama Linda.
To Cathy Singer: My conscience.
To Andre Duval: The yearbook.
To Ruth Yardum: My infinite gratitude and many more hours in the office.

Darls Centola

Chris Yardum

My plans are to attend Cal-State Northridge. And after that, who knows????

I, CHRIS YARDUM, Will to the following:

To Greg Miraglia: A Corvette Stingray

To Alison Gould: Fifty packs of bubble gum.

To Chuck Huenergardt: A Ferrari Boxer.

To Kathy Kenneally: A map of Australia, and a baby Koala bear.

To Darcy Dilley: Mike Havstead.

To Mike Havstad: The Termaline Queen Mine.

To Rose Cohen: A wall sized nude centerfold of George C. Scott.

To Edith Gay: A pair of roller skates to chase the kids on skateboards around, and say "Vite, Vite".

To Robin Duval: My body.

To my brother, John: A three liter engine for his Porsche.

To Andre Duval: I owe a great big "thank you" for helping my mother run the school, and for being sort of another father to me.

To my mother: I will always give her my love, and I don't know how to say that I'm so grateful for her caring about me so much.

Graduation will from Darls to Michael and La Toya

GRADUATING CLASS OF '75

I plan to further my education, go on to college, take business, then proceed onward in business law.

I, LA TOYA JACKSON, would like to Will the following:

To Cathy: The empty perfume bottles, the powdered white donuts, a year's supply of Dynamints, and all my skirts and dresses that fall below my knees.

To Michael: Another exciting and successful year at Cal-Prep.

To Greg: The best things in life.

To Darls: A beautiful garden filled with colorful birds, my wardrobe and my friendship.

La Toya Jackson

MID SEMESTER GRADUATE

My present plans are just to live and to finish my real estate brokerage license. My future plans are to study law and become a lawyer, also to get a degree in economics.

I, TIM BRIGGS, Will the following:

To Chuck Huenergardt: A German cross.

To Chris & John Yardum: My Cadillac, racers and club badge.

To Robin Duval: My Big Brotherhood.

To Rose Cohen: 26 novels all over 1000 pages.

To Andre Duval: Hazel.

To Mrs. Yardum: Happiness and Joy.

To the world: Peace, I hope.

Graduation will from La Toya to Michael and Darls

GRADUATING CLASS OF '75

I'm thinking about going into show business, but I'm not sure I'll like it.!! If I do like it, I'll continue.

I, MARLON JACKSON, Will to the following:

To my brother, Michael: All my class notes.
To my brother, Randy: The upper grade teachers.
To Michael Di Martini: All the assignments left for me when I go on a trip.
To Rose Cohen: An old shoe.
To Mike Havstad: His science speeches on cassette.

Marlon Jackson

I plan on going to Pierce College for two years, then to a University, hopefully out of state. I'll always remember my three years of school at Cal-Prep as happy ones.

Sue Soriano

I plan to go to college, don't know just where yet, and become a teacher.

I, JANIE FITZGERALD, Will by "extra credit" home-ec recipes to Juanita Armon and Jane Yardum.

Janie Fitzgerald

Graduation will from Marlon to Michael

Michael Jackson drawing for the yearbook

Who's Who

Categories	Guys	Gals
Most Sarcastic	Eric Schaeffer	Darcy Dilley
Most Studious	Greg Miraglia	Darls Centola
Sparkliest Eyes	Louis Miraglia	Robin Duval
Most Artistic	Michael Jackson	Julie Harb
Most Likely To Succeed	Chris Yardum Lenny Reeder	Darls Centola
Most Feminine/Masculine	Mark Cutter	La Toya Jackson
Best Sense of Humor	Larry Marks	Darcy Dilley
Foxiest	Mark Cutter	Nancy Flax
Most Liberal	Steve Hunio	Debbie Hammer
Best Actor/Actress	Scott Ashdown	Debbie Hammer
Most Rowdy	Bob Green	Christy Bono
Biggest Smile	Mark Bach	Kathy Kenneally
Longest Love Affair	Jim Caves	Joy Gessler
Best Dressed	Marlon Jackson	La Toya Jackson
Earthiest	Dave Hunt	Janie Fitzgerald
Most Enthusiastic	Scott Ashdown	Christy Bono
Straightest	Pete Shank	Cathy Singer
Biggest Show Off	Mark Bach	Debbie Lebowitz
Most Argumentative	Craig Ellis	Debbie Hammer
Most Athletic	Scott Ashdown	Debbie Alvarado
Most Quiet	Kurt Bellon	Nancy Morrison
Slyest	Mike Borkin Kelly Page	Darls Centola
Funniest Laugh	Kit Braun	Debbie Hammer

Who's Who list, 1975 yearbook
Notable entries include Michael, again voted
Most Artistic; and Darls, Most Likely to Succeed

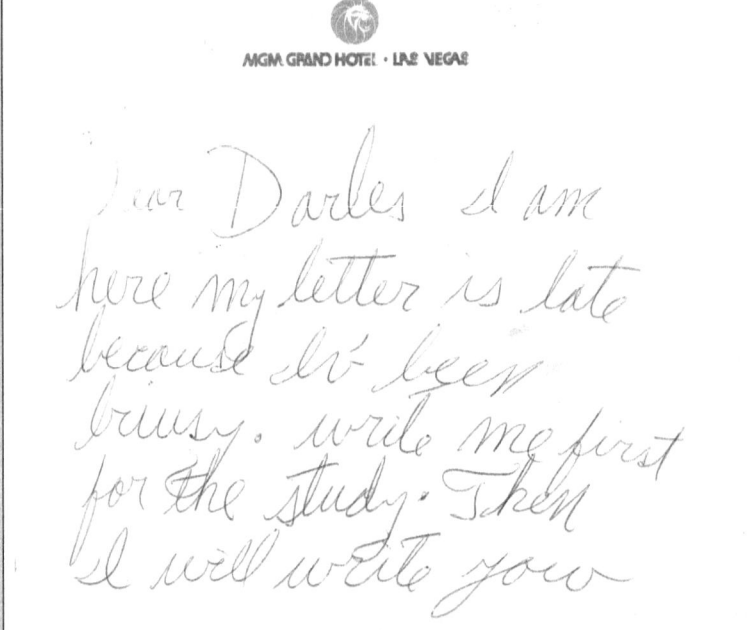

Long-distance Bible study letters between Michael and Darls

M.J.

Dear Darle,

I got your letter, but I got it a day late. And I have been busy that's why my letter is late.

I have bad news for you. You can't write me back. Because the house I am staying in doesn't have an adress. I am staying in a house on the lake. If you send the letter to the hotel it would never get in.

Sorry! But I am reading the book True Peace and Security that you gave to me.

The house we are staying in is beautiful. It looks like the old country side. it is a cabin house with steps upstairs, on the lake.

Keep on studying I have a big summer Tour. but I will keep studying.

over

Long-distance Bible study letters between Michael and Darls

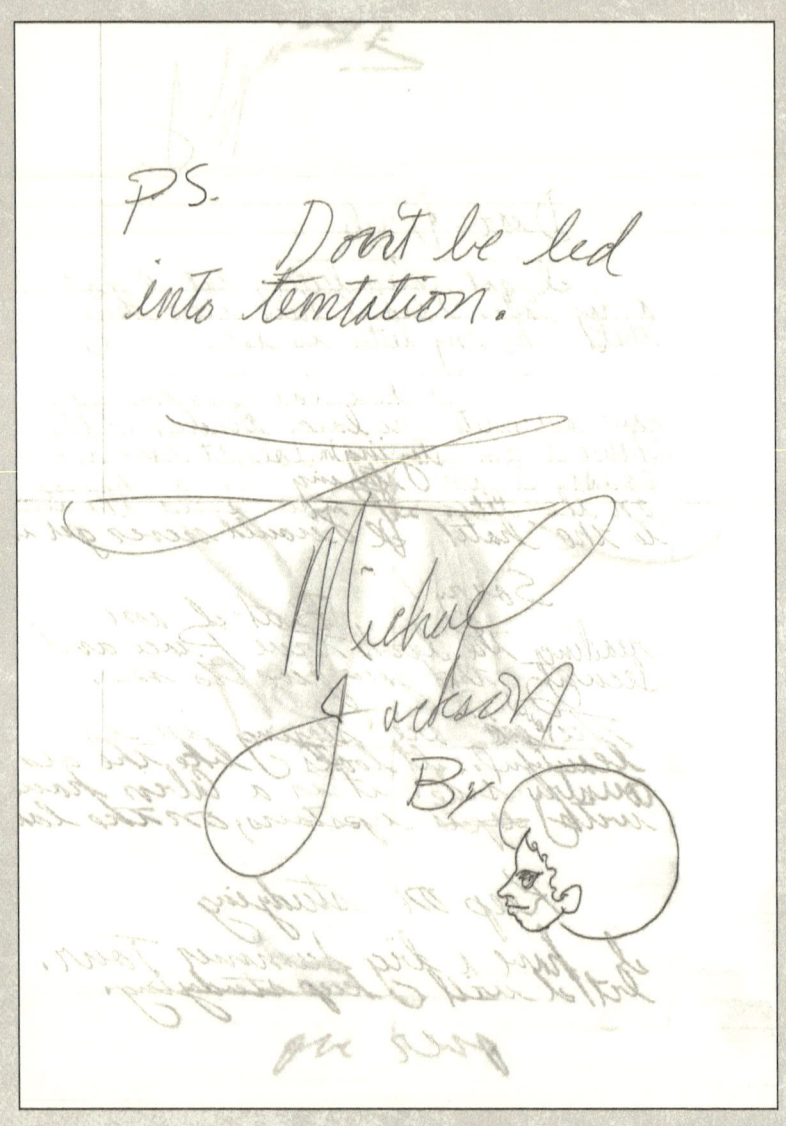

Jehovah's Witness slogan:
"Don't be led into temptation"

Envelopes from the MGM Grand Hotel in Las Vegas and the Sahara in Lake Tahoe, sent by Michael for long-distance Bible study with Darls

Black and white photo book gifted to Darls from Michael

> Look at this Darles as if they are your own children, Because they realy are you know
>
> love
> Michael Jackson
> 79

Michael's inscription in photo book

THE ENCYCLOPEDIA OF CHILD CARE AND GUIDANCE

REVISED EDITION

Sidonie Matsner Gruenberg, EDITOR

Frances Ullmann DeArmand, MANAGING EDITOR

Pauline Rush Evans, ASSOCIATE EDITOR

DOUBLEDAY & COMPANY, INC., GARDEN CITY, NEW YORK

Book gifted to Darls from Michael to honor their shared interest in working with children

> This is a great Book Darlene. You could realy use it in the future, never buy modern book's on children because the world gets crazier every -day. They tell you how to discipline your child psychologiesly and that's not good put this on in use. enjoy it
>
> Michey Jackson

An inscription inside of
The Encyclopedia of Child Care and Guidance

Wrapping paper with Michael's appreciation for our friendship

Bible study aid often used for new Jehovah's Witnesses

Darls Centola
4237 Longridge Ave.
North Hollywood, Calif. 91604

is a representative of the **WATCH TOWER BIBLE AND TRACT SOCIETY OF PENNSYLVANIA**, Brooklyn, N.Y., and is authorized to preach the gospel of Jehovah's kingdom from house to house under the direction of the

CONGREGATION OF JEHOVAH'S WITNESSES

G. Carleidas (Presiding Minister)   9-7-74 date issued

S-65   Printed in U.S.A.

(Signature) Darls Centola

NO BLOOD TRANSFUSION!

As a God-fearing Christian and a believer in Jehovah God and his Word, the Bible, I hereby demand that blood in any way, shape or form, is NOT to be fed into my body. "You must not eat the blood of any sort of flesh." (Leviticus 17:14) Please read the following texts in the Bible: Genesis 9:4; Leviticus 17:11, 12; Deuteronomy 12:23; Acts 15:20, 28, 29; 21:25. However, non-blood alternatives may be used if necessary.

Signature: _Darls Centola_

Baptized Jehovah's Witnesses carry this identification indicating "No Blood Transfusion!" based on Scripture

"Proving our faith to be alive by works"
— Jas. 2:26

My Goal is 20 hrs

I have lots to go

❖{ The Present Need }❖

Be not heedful of the morrow, but rather gaze upon today, for sufficient for today is the miracle thereof.

Be not overmindful of yourself when you give but be mindful of the necessity. For every giver himself receives from the Father, and that much more abundantly.

hrs	Date		Lit.	Date
1 hr. 15 mins Serv.	1	1 hr. S/C 24	4 mag. Secu.	1
1 hr. st.w/B	9	2 hr. Serv. 25	6 mag serv.	25
1½ hr. st.w/C	10	13	1 mag L.T.	23
1 hr. st w/m	14	2 hr. st.w/c+m 27		
1 hr. st w/c	14	1 hr. 28 w/m		
½ hr. st/w m:	15	½ hr. 30		
1 hr. st w/m	16	½ w/m 31		
3½ hr. ~~Serv~~ w/c.	20	extra 15 min.		
1 hr. w/m;C	21	⑰ hrs.		
1 hr. w/m;C LT.	22			
½ hr. text	20, -22			

Bible Study Log

Page from journal logging Bible study hours with Michael and literature sold

ACKNOWLEDGMENTS

First and foremost, to **Michael Jackson**—thank you for empowering me to find my own truth.

To **La Toya Jackson**, for her precious friendship and example of courage.

Cheerleaders, Coaches, and Mentors
Your guidance, encouragement, and belief in my voice have been invaluable:
- William Janiec
- Karin Gutman and *Spirit of Story*
- Rachel Langer
- Lisa Doctor
- Skye Orloski
- Robert Morgan Fisher
- David Wogahn
- Manon Wogahn
- Michael Jackson Facebook Book Club
- Christie Strong
- Christian Volk
- Jennifer Laine

- Zuzanna and Campbell Wilson and Rocinante Studios
- Alice Bradley

Friends and Early Readers

Thank you for reading my words when they were raw and for your honest and valuable input. Thank you, too, for your warm support and endless patience.

- My siblings: Angela Centola, Lisa Ocheltree, Susie Centola, and Michael Centola
- Lori Chapman
- Wendy Ashley
- Robin Duval
- Frankie Janiec
- Maggie Lynch
- Janice Hill
- Jane Garnett
- J. Ashley T. Booth
- Miles Johnstone
- Pat Brown
- Maggie Darcey Schifferdecker
- Susanna de Mari

To My Clients

I am deeply grateful to the courageous clients I've worked with over the years—you have taught me so much about the human spirit, resilience, and the many ways people respond to spiritual abuse. Your stories, your vulnerability, and your willingness to heal have shaped my understanding and inspired this work more than you know.

RESOURCES FOR ADVERSE RELIGIOUS EXPERIENCES

Adverse Religious Experiences refer to any religious belief, practice, or structure that undermines a person's sense of safety, autonomy, or well-being—whether physical, emotional, social, relational, sexual, or psychological. These experiences can result in religious trauma.

Common abuses include community violence, bullying, threats, intimidation, public outing, stigmatizing, forced confessions, shunning, brainwashing, isolation, information control, scapegoating, identity disruption, emotional manipulation, phobia induction, dress and behavior control, segregation, and love bombing or trauma bonding.

Healing from high-control religious trauma involves restoring safety to the nervous system, critically examining imposed beliefs, dismantling external conditioning, and moving toward empowered resolution.

Books:
- *Leaving the Witness: Exiting a Religion and Finding a Life*, Amber Scorah
- *Confessions of a Teenage Jesus Jerk*, Tony DuShane
- *You Lied to Me About God: A Memoir*, Jamie Marich, PhD
- *When Religion Hurts You: Healing From Religious Trauma and the Impact of High-Control Religion*, Laura E. Anderson, PhD
- *The Myth of Normal: Trauma, Illness, & Healing in a Toxic Culture*, Gabor Maté, MD with Daniel Maté
- *The Body Keeps the Score: Brain, Mind, and Body in the Healing of Trauma*, Bessel van der Kolk
- *Separation of Church and Hate: A Sane Person's Guide to Taking Back the Bible from Fundamentalists, Fascists, and Flock-Fleecing Frauds*, John Fugelsang

More Resources:
- **The International Cultic Studies Association (ICSA)**
A non-profit educational and anti-cult organization, provides resources and information on cults and cultic groups, focusing on the intensity of psychosocial influence within groups, rather than solely on the label "cult."
www.icsahome.com
- **Center for Trauma Resolution and Recovery**
This is a group of trauma-informed practitioners from across the United States who utilize the medium of coaching to provide access to trauma resolu-

tion and recovery to clients all over the world. Their online format makes it easy to receive the support you're looking for as you begin or continue healing from trauma, no matter your time zone or schedule.
www.traumaresolutionandrecovery.com

- **Religious Trauma Therapist Directory**
The Reclamation Collective is a 501c3 organization centering survivors of religious trauma and spiritual abuse by curating virtual support groups for those navigating deconstruction and reclamation on their healing trajectory. We additionally house a religious trauma informed clinician directory on our website, where folks can find a therapist licensed in the state or province where they reside.
www.reclamationcollective.com/find-a-therapist-1

- **Emily Hedrick** is a Consultant and Coach who help survivors of toxic religious cultures and toxic workplace environments get back in touch with who they truly want to be. That includes working specifically with religious trauma and compassion fatigue.
https://emilyhedrickcoachingandconsulting.com/can-spiritual-abuse-cause-ptsd

ABOUT THE AUTHOR

DARLS CENTOLA, LCSW, is a Los Angeles–based trauma therapist, author, and educator with more than 25 years of experience working with the impacts of spiritual abuse and high-control systems. A former Jehovah's Witness who walked away to reclaim her autonomy, she brings both lived experience and clinical expertise to her work—specializing in EMDR, Internal Family Systems, and trauma-informed care. Before becoming a therapist, she worked as a sign language interpreter, a European tour guide, and a high school teacher. She holds a master's degree in social work from the University of Hawai'i and lives by the beach in Los Angeles, California. *Finding Truth with Michael* is her first book. Learn more at www.FindingTruthWithMichael.com.

www.ingramcontent.com/pod-product-compliance
Lightning Source LLC
LaVergne TN
LVHW091717070526
838199LV00050B/2440